Murl Salmon

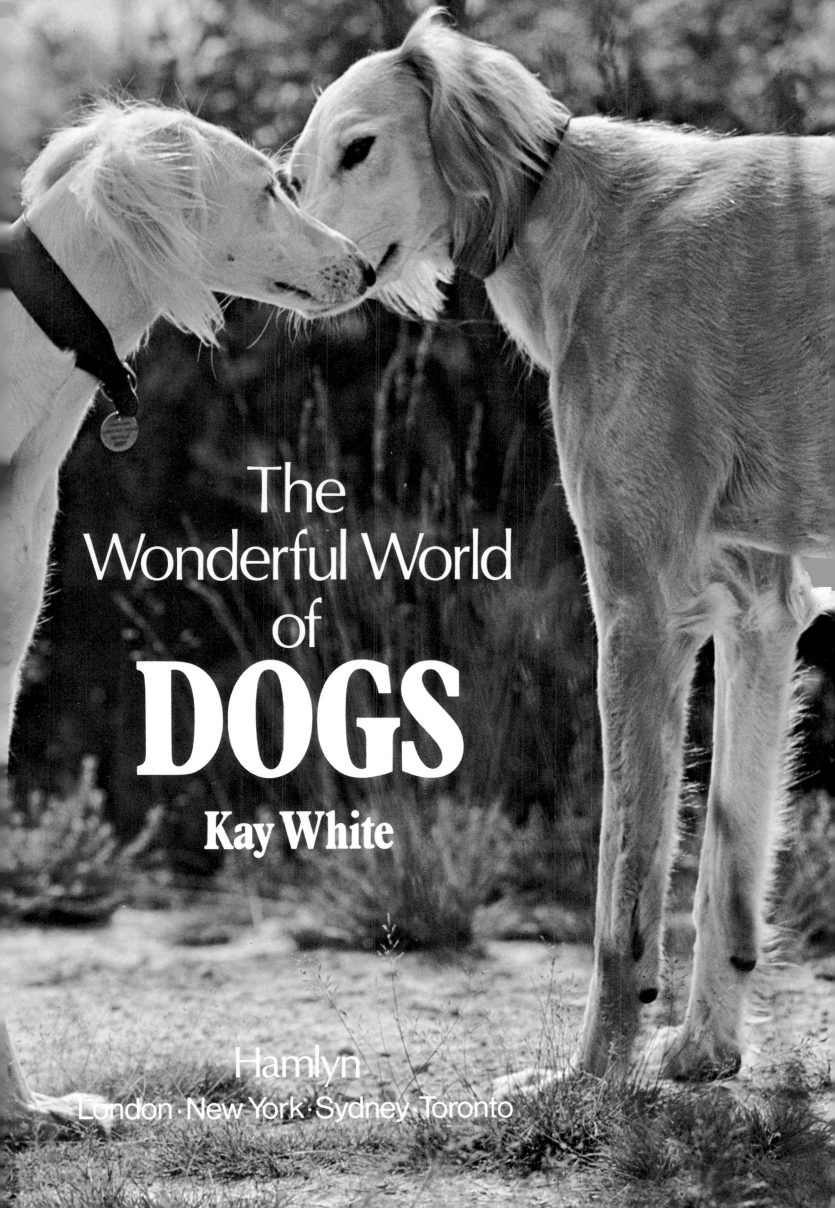

The Wonderful World of DOGS

Kay White

HAMLYN
London · New York · Sydney · Toronto

Published by
The Hamlyn Publishing Group Limited
London · New York · Sydney · Toronto
Astronaut House, Feltham, Middlesex, England
Copyright © The Hamlyn Publishing Group Limited 1976
ISBN 0 600 37111 5

Filmset in England by Keyspools Limited, Golborne, Lancs.
Printed in Holland

Contents

Introduction 6

Choosing your dog 7

Dog care 9

Which breed? 10

Hounds 11

Gundogs 23

Working dogs 36

Terriers 54

Utility dogs 66

Toy dogs 77

Other varieties 88

Acknowledgments 96

Introduction

For thousands of years man has regarded the dog as a necessary part of his life, as a working and a sporting partner, as a guard and as a companion. The desire to own a dog is as strong as ever today and many people look forward with happy anticipation to the day when they will have a suitable home or more leisure to enjoy the company of a dog. Sadly, in the last quarter of the twentieth century, many factors seem to be combining to make the dog a luxury which many must forego. The conflicting desires for freedom of action and for women to work outside the home makes it impossible to provide the companionship a dog needs. City flats and out-of-town, open-plan estates prove to be unsuitable places for pet owners. The intensive use of farming land and preservation of the countryside restrict the available exercise ground, while fast motor traffic means that all exercise must be supervised.

Loneliness is a twentieth-century problem for the solitary and the elderly, but with the pull of opportunities for holidays and club activities, those who need a dog most have to sacrifice outings for the joy of a full-time, wagging tail.

A pet as playmate and confidant may be the salvation of a lonely child with busy parents and an environment which changes too often. Children learn much from having a dog in the family, from the need to give care and consideration to something of less status than themselves, to the acceptance of illness, death and mourning when a pet dies.

Pets should never be acquired lightly and later 'given away' or 'sent back to kennels'. While death can be accepted, after illness, accident or old age, getting rid of something that is awkward, a burden or slow to learn and given to making mistakes can have terrible implications in the mind of a child who knows that it is easy for him to fail in these ways himself.

Adult households need a dog too, as a care object, perhaps as a topic of conversation when all else fails. Inhibitions about bodily contact, touching and stroking vanish when there is a dog for patting and stroking, bouncing and wrestling, and for playing youthful games which would look foolish alone. One of the dog's virtues is that it can, within reasonable limits, be turned off to suit our mood, without the need of explanation and excuses.

If we still want to keep a dog at a time when many protests are made that the dog is an antisocial nuisance, our animals must be kept in such a way that they do not cause annoyance to others. This will mean keeping a dog of suitable size and character within a well-fenced area, and only allowing the dog out when in charge of an adult with full control of the dog. The dog must not be confined for long periods without company so that it barks and whines. We must make sure it does not foul pavements or let it spoil others' enjoyment of public places. Above all, it means not buying unwisely and then discarding the dog—the number of unwanted dogs destroyed annually is a great reproach to so-called dog lovers. The contented dog in surroundings appropriate to size and breed is easy to control. The noisy, destructive and aggressive animal is basically unhappy through lack of anyone to care enough to impose discipline. I hope that this book may help you to choose your dog wisely; the rewards are great for those that can provide all that is meant by 'a good home'.

Choosing your dog

Your first step in caring for a dog properly is to buy a healthy puppy which has had the best care in the first few weeks of its life. Dog psychologists working in America have proved that the attitude of the bitch towards human beings greatly influences the temperament of her pups. The way the puppies are handled, between the ages of three and nine weeks is crucial in forming their future characters. Feeding and care of the dam and the sire are important in influencing the quality of the offspring, as well as correct weaning and worming, and acclimatization to all the experiences a puppy is likely to meet as a family pet. A recent veterinary survey proved convincingly that the healthiest puppies are those reared by specialist dog breeders and bought direct from the premises on which they were born. In Britain, owners of more than two breeding bitches are now licensed by their local authority. Their premises must then be always open to inspection by Environmental Health Officers. Dealing with a licensed kennel assures you that the housing, feeding and general care has reached a satisfactory standard, but gives no warranty for the health of a litter of puppies.

The alternative place to purchase is from a pet shop or dog dealer, recognizable by constant advertisements for many breeds of puppies. These pups will not have been born on the premises, indeed, the vendor will probably not have seen the parents of the litters, which are bought by agents from the owners.

The specialist breeder can tell you much about the ancestors of your pup, and will probably advise and help you all through its life. You may have to seek out a breeder, and most likely wait for a puppy, but it will be worth waiting for in the long term. Lists of breeders may be obtained from the kennel clubs of all countries, from specialist dog fancy papers and sporting magazines.

Sympathy and sentiment run high when looking at puppies; there is often a kindly impulse to give a home to a small, weak or deformed pup. Please harden your heart, for it is a mistaken kindness. Substandard puppies which are cheap because of doubts about their health can prove to be the most expensive of the lot. One reason for being particularly selective about the family puppy is the risk that some diseases are transmitted to humans. Children may become infected by worm larvae shed by puppies and it is possible for humans to contract enteritis or brucellosis. In households where the standard of hygiene is high the risk is minimal, but there is no sense in weighting the odds by taking an unhealthy puppy.

This miniature Dachshund is willing to let the photographer approach her puppies, but all the same gives a wary look. All bitches are very protective of their puppies, and will go to great lengths to hide them if they feel the pups are threatened by strangers around their home.

When you inspect a litter of puppies, they should have no disagreeable odour, and the faeces should be formed and firm, not foul nor explosive. Eyes should be bright, the nose and mouth clean, and the pups should be moving on all four legs by the age of twenty-four to twenty-eight days. There should be no hernias at the navel or the groin, ears should be clean, and the coat springy and lively. Try to see all the litter, even if some are booked, and do not tolerate the vendor who will show you only one puppy at a time and does not introduce the dam. The bitch may well look thin, with scratched mammary glands and a patchy coat after rearing a big litter, but she should look well cared for and happy, her comforts attended to, and she should be as friendly as befits her breed character. The puppies should be housed in adequate warmth, or shade, with ample room to get away from their bed for defecation – puppies reared in overcrowded conditions are not easy to housetrain. Your final safeguard is to state that you will take the puppy for a veterinary check, which must be done on the day you collect the puppy or at the latest the morning after. If there is some defect which makes the puppy unsuitable as a companion dog, you should get a certificate from the vet stating his reasons for the decision. You then have every right to return the pup to the breeder and get your money refunded and you are not obliged to take another dog in exchange.

All breeds of dog, and crossbreds too, may develop a hereditary defect or illness, impossible to see in a young puppy. No one can give a warranty of lifelong health for a dog, nor can a breeder vow that your pup will be of pleasant temperament, as irritable or shy individuals occur from the best-natured parents.

Which sex will you choose? In the larger breeds, males are heavier and more forceful, needing more control than females. If you want your dog to travel and take part in sports or activities with the family, the male is more available, as the bitch will be out of action during her oestrus periods. These occur for the first time before she is a year old, and afterwards at six- to eight-month intervals, lasting roughly three weeks at a time. There is not yet a long-term contraceptive pill for the bitch, only a hormone preparation which delays oestrus, but cannot be used continually. Veterinary surgeons have some reservations about spaying, or performing a hysterectomy, on a bitch just to make her more convenient to own, for if the operation is done while the bitch is still a puppy, there may be personality changes and immaturity of the sexual organs and she may become lethargic and dull. Vasectomies may be performed on male dogs, making them infertile but not destroying their urge to mate or the desire to mark their territory with a stream of urine. Castration of the male alters the personality.

This Labrador is delivering game to hand, not at the sit, as expected in obedience trials, but in a way perfectly acceptable to his sporting owner. Good manners are essential to the shooter's dog; a dog that runs in to game, or interferes with other animals makes its owner very unpopular.

Dog Care

Most companion dogs are fed too well, at too great expense. Obesity commonly shortens the pet animal's life, and a diet over-rich in meat predisposes it to kidney disease in middle-age. The dog requires only twenty-two percent protein, but, of course, easily becomes addicted to meat and will demand more if indulged. The ideal diet is fifty percent meat, fish, cheese, or cooked egg, and fifty percent carbohydrate, in the form of biscuit meal, or stale brown bread. The meat or fish element contains fibre, fat and water as well as protein. The meat given may be fresh meat, raw or cooked, tinned dog meat, or a deep-frozen product.

If fresh meat is used, a carefully measured allowance of a balanced vitamin and mineral supplement should be added, but leading brands of tinned meat have the vitamin content replaced after cooking. Over-vitaminization, especially with cod-liver oil (vitamin D) causes bone deformity.

The most modern way of feeding is to use an air-dried diet, containing soya protein. This clean-to-handle, biscuit-style feed contains all the nutritive elements a dog needs, but up to twenty percent of meat and fish as flavouring may be added in the form of household scraps. Some adult dogs like a milk drink, while others find it too laxative and some are allergic to milk products. No dog needs sugar or chocolate.

When you have your puppy, your first task is to find out from a veterinary surgeon the programme for preventative inoculations, which have so largely removed the dread of distemper from dog owners' lives. All puppies, pedigreed or crossbred, should be immunized by the time they are three months old, and should not be taken out in public places before the immunization is effective. Housetraining starts directly you have the pup in your home, but in excessively bad weather you may decide to continue to allow the dog to use a pad of newspaper indoors, as it will have been trained as a puppy to do. Housetraining consists of watching the pup, taking it outside, and staying with it until it performs, for it will not teach itself by being shut outside the back door. Puppies should be played with, and talked to, but allowed a great deal of undisturbed sleep during the day. The constantly agitated young dog grows up fractious and nervy. Do not allow children to pounce upon a puppy suddenly or to squeal at it, as the dog's hearing and sense of alarm are very keen. Teach the dog from the first to stay alone for periods of ten minutes or so, but it is expecting too much to make a puppy stay all night alone in a strange new home. Take it to your bedroom, or sleep downstairs until the new member of the family has complete confidence in its surroundings. This preliminary support reinforces your position as the pup's new pack leader, to whom it looks for discipline and leadership. On this basis, you can teach a dog all you will ever want of it.

This Boxer bitch is teaching her puppy play-fighting. The puppy taken from the nest too young misses much of the benefit of maternal training in how to be a dog. Dams teach their puppies how to play, how to attack an enemy and how to defend themselves by quick evasive tactics. Notice the docked tail held erect and the well-angled hind legs on the pup.

Which Breed?

The many distinct breeds which we know today have been isolated by selection of animals for a physical characteristic, or special ability which man could use. In the early civilizations a dog which was of special use in hunting or catching animals for food was a worthy possession. Later, when cattle and flocks were the mainstay of a community, the dog that would warn and guard against intruders also earned its keep. When the pursuit of game became more of a sport, the cleverest, or most useful dog was envied by the other participants. Throughout our history, we have altered and developed the dog, cultivating the tall, agile hound for hunting prey by sight over long distances, and the lower-built animals with wide nostrils and acute scent powers for smaller game; the massive dogs with broad muzzles made the best guards and fighters; the sharp little killers the best rodent eradicators; the diminutive and dwarfed specimens the best household pets and toys. In conjunction with physical attributes, dogs adapted by temperamental inclination. These strong instincts persist and cannot be completely trained out even through many generations as domestic pets. In choosing a dog as a family or personal companion it is essential to be aware of the breed's natural behaviour, as this may sometimes make your choice difficult to live with, even though you continue to admire its physical beauty.

The kennel clubs hold the standards of the breeds and make dog show regulations, the classification varying a little between countries. The general headings of hounds, terriers, toys, gundogs, utility and working apply all over the world, with minor differences – for example, the toy Poodle is a toy dog in USA, but classified with the miniature and standard as a utility dog in Britain. The Basenji is a hound in USA and Britain, but classified as a spitz or Nordic dog in Scandinavia. Not all breeds have official recognition in each country, breeds tending to be strongest in their country of origin, although the necessity, in World War II, of sending many fine British and European dogs to USA, where the food situation was easier, gave that country a wonderful opportunity to build up superlative kennels in many breeds, which have since sent the descendants across the Atlantic again.

Above
Grooming must be a daily ritual for the long-haired dog. They must be taught from puppy days to sit, lie or roll over on command so that the toilet is a restful interlude and not a battle between dog and owner. Some types of dog hair may be collected and spun for weaving or knitting into garments.

Right
Doing what comes naturally, this crossbred terrier is enjoying a good scratch. Scratching is not always indicative of fleas or other skin irritation. The dog sometimes scratches from embarrassment, as a tactful backdown from a confrontation with an enemy, or to deflect an order which it is unwilling to obey.

Hounds

The Saluki moving gracefully over the sand shows all the fastidious elegance of its kind. The slender legs are lifted in a well-flexed trot, the head is held high in typical gaze hound manner, and the balancing tail which gives flexibility in the turn, ends in a characteristic circle. Any colour combination is permitted in the Saluki.

The hounds divide into two types: those like the Greyhound and the Afghan which hunt by sight, pursuing their quarry with speed and agility; and the slower, thickset Basset and Beagle which hunt by scent, and hardly use their eyes at all.

The sight or gaze hounds date back to about 3000 BC when the Greyhound type of dog was depicted in Egyptian art. The descendants of these dogs are still recognizable in the Afghan, Borzoi, Deerhound, Greyhound, Wolfhound, Saluki and Whippet. Elegance is a joint virtue, with a nobility of bearing and an aloof coolness as the hallmark of aristocratic ancestry. The gaze hounds are not eager, or busy, they do not bounce or agitate, and in the home they can be very restful and undemanding. Their disadvantage as companions is the difficulty of allowing them any free exercise in safe places, and some owners may regret that these hounds do not show exuberant affection. Gaze hounds are not readily obedient, so they must be exercised in a well-fenced area, and the garden in which they spend their leisure should be enclosed up to a height of 6 feet (2 metres), with the lower 1 foot (0·3 metre) buried in concrete, as agile hounds both jump and dig. Freedom and fast galloping over considerable distances are essential to their physical well-being, but they are seldom safe with smaller dogs or cats, as their basic instinct is to chase other fur.

If you keep a gaze hound, you must spend a lot of time in constructive play, allowing it to dart, weave and turn in the chase so that strong muscles are developed, with agility and hard condition. Puppies up to six months, in hounds in common with other large breeds, must not be exhausted, and will not seem too exacting in their requirements at that time, but from adolescence, owning a gaze hound of which you can be proud involves time and effort. They are not dogs to be incorporated in the family with minimal trouble. The breed virtue of quickness can also mean disaster, for a loose hound in a town runs great risk from traffic, and in the country it may do a great deal of damage to stock. Too much confinement in a small house will lead to destructive behaviour from sheer boredom. Hounds are usually tolerant of children, but not very playful and they should never be sent out in the charge of children, and never tied up outside shops in case the temptation of a passing poodle proves too great.

The Afghan Hound in full glory of show coat, the long silky hair covering the body from the neat centre forehead parting right down to the lavishly furnished paws, is a very glamorous creature indeed, although this show outfit would not allow the hound to gallop anywhere, as it would fall over its own foot fringes. Even with the coat trimmed down, time must be spent at least twice a week on grooming very thoroughly, working with the coat slightly damp to avoid breaking the hair. Dead hair tends to mat in the coat, so tangles must be carefully teased out, and feet must be washed daily if they are not to become balled up with mud.

The Saluki shares a common ancestry with the Afghan, having the same attributes of grace, speed and agility, with the symmetry of form more easily appreciated as the coat is short and silky except for feathering on ears, legs and tail. There is the same dignity and gentle bearing, and perhaps rather more attachment to its owner in this royal dog of Egypt, the oldest known domesticated

dog. Desert tribes used the Saluki to bring down gazelle, moving at up to 50 miles an hour (80·5 kilometres an hour). In Britain, Saluki owners enjoy the sport of hare coursing, and will probably adapt to the American sport of lure coursing in a stadium if live-hare sport is forbidden by law.

The Greyhound is primarily the dog of the racetrack, a most popular spectator sport in Britain and USA, where it originated. In racing, speed and fitness count for much, and sentiment not at all, so that any unprosperous dog is culled, rendering the Greyhound remarkably free from hereditary disease. Owning a racing Greyhound is an expensive business, as it must remain in training kennels all the time it is raced, although owners may visit on Sundays. Most racing dogs are retired at four years, and then they must be retrained to domestic life and taught house manners. There is a wide divergence in the racing and show type of Greyhound, and hardly any are dual purpose. Greyhounds are specifically banned from free running in some city parks, and in others they must be muzzled. Like all the gaze hounds they will chase and kill smaller dogs and cats, so proving a liability in an urban situation if not controlled.

The Whippet, a smaller edition of the Greyhound, is known as the poor man's sporting dog, but the popularity of this charming breed is spreading far beyond the workmen of northern Britain who are traditionally credited with the cult of the Whippet. The English Kennel Club standard allows for a smaller dog than the American, which permits the male to be 22 inches (0·56 metres) at the shoulder. The Whippet is affectionate and gentle, very clean in the home, and charming to own, provided normal hound precautions are taken.

The Irish Wolfhound and the Scottish Deerhound come from similar stock, although the Irish hound is the larger, the tallest of all dogs, standing over 36 inches (0·9 metres) at the shoulder. An imposing dog with nobility and quiet, composed behaviour, sheer size makes the Wolfhound unsuitable for most families, although several hundred are kept in Britain, and USA where they are used for coursing coyote. Fionn, mascot of the Irish Guards, wins admiration for his dignity and patience whenever he is seen on ceremonial parade with his regiment.

The Scottish Deerhound was owned exclusively by the king's companions in medieval times. They used the dogs to bring down stags in highland country. This powerful and agile hound is all gentleness in the home; it cannot tolerate rough treatment and harsh words. Size and room to exercise are the drawbacks to owning a Deerhound, as well as the expense of feeding and boarding so large a dog.

Until Victorian times, the Borzoi was the hound of the Russian aristocracy. It was made popular in Britain by Queen Alexandra, consort of King Edward VII. This graceful hound is very sensitive, not easily friendly with strangers and a problem to exercise. The breed has some hereditary tendency to pyloric disfunction ('bloat'), if not managed and fed with great care, so the Borzoi is something of a specialist's dog and not really suitable as pet of a busy family.

The Basenji is the hunting dog of the Sudan and Zaire, a small-sized dog whose erect ears give super-acute hearing. Inside the house the Basenji is a joy, as it cleans its fur like a cat. Outside it is more of a problem, as obedience is not its strong point. A mischievous, fascinating companion, the Basenji yodels in conversational tones instead of barking.

Hounds of the Bloodhound, Basset and Beagle type hunt by scent. They are of heavier and lower build, speed being a disadvantage for their work, but they typically have wide nostrils, pendulous ears and deep flews around the mouth. All the scent hounds bay, bark or what is known as 'give tongue' to help fellow pack members. Hunting folk speak of it as music, but your neighbours may not!

The Bloodhound is a very large dog indeed, a one-man rather than a family dog. A superlative tracker, it is cruel not to provide this hound with some work, even if it is only organized trail finding at club events. The Bloodhound must have a very steady regime, regular times of feeding twice daily and no exercise after meals, owing to a breed tendency to 'bloat'.

The Basset Hound has rocketed to popularity since it was featured in advertisements, although this has attracted owners to the breed who look for qualities these hounds do not possess. The Basset is a slow thinker on its own, stubborn, a little stolid, and not quick to catch on to any idea, even housetraining. Great care is needed in rearing a Basset puppy, to build the huge bone and firm muscle necessary to the shape, while preventing injury to the shoulder and crooked front legs. The Basset is an outdoor dog, happiest with a companion of its own kind and a well-ordered life which does not put too great a strain on its powers of thought.

The Beagle is another pack hound which has lately caught the public's fancy as a pet. Reasonably sized and short-coated, with a merry disposition, the Beagle is easy to feed and has a good bark to warn intruders. In common with other pack hounds, Beagles are slow to housetrain, but usually they are of genial temperament and love children.

These young Bloodhounds show the long, narrow head which gives them such unique sniff-power. The skin around the eyes falls in loose folds, the ears hang low falling forward when the dog has its head to the ground and obscuring the eyes, but the hound's nose tells it all it needs to know. Bloodhounds are usually black and tan in colour. When fully grown they are very heavy dogs, usually of very good temperament but with a deep baying bark which does not encourage the approach of strangers.

Right
Following a scent is the most natural instinct of the Beagle, as these eight-week-old puppies show, with their heads down, ears falling forward, and tails just a little uncertain in angle. Almost any colour or markings are acceptable in the breed, these being tri-colours and red and whites.

Below
This dog is waiting at the 'down' for the next order. Obedience training does not come easily to the Beagle, but some owners enjoy the challenge of working with an unusual breed. All competitors must perform the same routine and are marked with the same severity as the border collies and Alsatians which take to obedience naturally.

The Dachshund, or German Teckel, is a low-slung, long-bodied dog bred to go to ground after badger and hare. The qualities of courage and determination in the chase and the ability to give tongue to indicate their location now emerge in a hound of strong character, which can be obstinate, determined, and given to bouts of persistent barking. The Dachshund in two sizes, standard at a maximum of 20 pounds (9 kilograms) and 10 pounds (4.5 kilograms) for miniatures, at the British Kennel Club, and with three coat textures, is popular the world over, the miniatures being most in demand. The Dachs can be greedy, and the comical sight of its long body and imploring paws balanced by the tail, begging for titbits, often undermines the resolve of owners not to overfeed. This is such a pity, as the fat Dachs is not healthy and will have a shortened life with little natural enjoyment. Dachs are still very much hounds, and will dig and wriggle their way out of a garden to follow an interesting scent. As a puppy, a Dachs is a responsibility, as it must not be allowed to play on steps or steep banks for fear of stretching the shoulder muscles and making the front ugly. Exaggerated length of back has resulted in a tendency to weakness of the spine, with spontaneous disc protrusion, giving acute pain and subsequent paralysis and incontinence, but many hounds make good recoveries with careful nursing and rest.

The Pharaoh Hound has retained its ancient shape, being exactly similar now to the bas-relief murals found in Egyptian tombs. These hounds are very pure blooded, having been bred on the islands of Gozo and Malta for 2,000 years. A hound which hunts by scent and sight, having very acute hearing and a great turn of speed, the Pharaoh does not miss very much that goes on around its home. A very beautiful animal, it is a little difficult to own, owing to the problem of providing safe exercise.

The Norwegian Elkhound is unlike the other hounds in physical shape, but has adapted superbly to its native rugged terrain and sub-zero temperatures. The Elkhound was bred to track, and hold the elk at bay until the huntsmen came up, producing a brave and powerful dog which must have sensible domination from puppy days. The coat requires a daily brush, and when the undercoat is shed, it makes quite a mess in the house.

The Rhodesian Ridgeback is a composite hound, with Greyhound and Mastiff in its make up, bred specifically to hunt lions in Africa. This is a large dog, around 80 pounds (36 kilograms) in weight, but for the right household the Ridgeback can be a great success, being gentle in manner with children but a strong guard against intruders. Have a vet check a Ridgeback puppy for hereditary dermoid sinus – a small opening in the neck region which penetrates to the spinal cord and will never heal.

The Coonhound is an exclusively American breed, owing a lot to the Bloodhounds imported from Britain to Virginia in the seventeenth century. These hounds are kept to hunt raccoon at night, their strong scenting ability and melodious call enabling them to work in the dark and firmly indicate the tree holding a raccoon. These are pack hounds, not kept in the home, or very much exhibited. There is none at present in Britain.

Below
This Greyhound shows all the physical attributes which make the breed so fleet and agile: the long head; neat ears and eyes set obliquely; powerful, pointed jaws; deep chest with plenty of room for lung expansion; flexible hind quarters on narrow loins to give quick turning ability and a long tail for balance.

Left
This chestnut and white Borzoi stands 32 inches (81 centimetres) at the shoulder, every inch an aristocrat. The head is long and finely chiselled, and the jaw has a scissors bite. The back is long and slightly curved, and the sickle-shaped tail is carried low. The British and American standards allow all colours, but Continental judges prefer light-coloured dogs.

Right
This Whippet shows all the elegance and grace of its kind. The head is wide between the eyes, which are bright, intelligent and full of devotion. The chest is deep, giving plenty of lung room, and the back is long, to allow the dog to cover a lot of ground when galloping.

These three Dachshund heads show the three coat types, while the facial expressions give some hint of the characters that go with the different coats. The smooth-haired dog has a bold, challenging, inquisitive expression. The head is long and tapering to the nose, clean and sharp in outline. The dark brown eyes are oval in shape, set obliquely with a clear lively, friendly gaze.

The long-haired Dachs is the same in shape, but covered in silky hair, long on the ears, and with feathering on legs and tail. The long-hairs are more wily, more ingratiating than the smooths, betraying something of their spaniel ancestry. The wire-haired Dachs has a short, harsh coat, bushy eyebrows and a beard on the chin. Something in the attitude of the wire-haired in the picture is reminiscent of the Dandie Dinmont Terrier, with which the smooth Dachs was crossed to produce the wire-coated dog, with a more durable coat for working in rough country covered in gorse and thorny undergrowth.

Right
This black and tan Coonhound is called 'Lyrical Treeboy', a very apt name for a hound whose work is to bark at the foot of trees, holding racoon and opossum while the hunters follow on foot. This hound shows much of the Bloodhound characteristics from which this American breed was developed.

Below
These Rhodesian Ridgebacks show the marked ridge of hair, growing in reverse direction to the main coat, which runs down the centre back of the dog, ending correctly in two whorls. The back is long and muscular and the colour always a shade of red with small white markings on chest and paws.

Right
A totally different shape from the speed hounds, the Elkhound is heavy in shoulder to facilitate its work of pulling loads. The attractive colouring is grey with black tips to the guard hairs. This dog shows the correct forward-looking eye; an oblique eye or falling ears loses show points.

Below
This Afghan Hound is in superb show coat, its ears well feathered and the long hair extending right down to the feet. Notice the haunch bones which stand out correctly, and the tail curved up at the tip. A lot of time must be spent every day to keep this dog so well groomed.

Above
The Deerhound is a little smaller than the Wolfhound, rather lighter in build and showing Greyhound influence. Notice the long back, and the tail which is carried down in a graceful curve when the dog is standing. When galloping the tail is carried to continue the line of the back. Ears are set high and folded back, always dark on every coat colour.

Right
These kind and gentle giants are Irish Wolfhounds. They show the correct heavily boned, straight front legs, and strong, well-arched necks carrying the head proudly. The coat is wiry and the eyes are dark. The body is long and the hindquarters show great power and capacity for speed, although on a lead at the walk the Wolfhound is very docile.

Gundogs

As the hound was bred to chase game in open country, so the gundog was developed to flush birds out of woodland, indicate birds sitting in the open, and retrieve those that fell. An essential assistant to filling the larder at one time, it now provides sport for shooting men. The natural attributes of some of the gundogs have made them suitable for more sophisticated duties with the army, police and customs officers, as gundogs can be taught to track out drugs, explosives and other animals which may be smuggled in to a country. The gundogs also provide the majority of the guides for blind persons.

In the Middle Ages, dogs would flush out game for the mounted huntsman to kill with the hawk. A dog was also essential when game was netted, when two men would draw a net over the back of a crouching or setting dog which was indicating the position of a covey, which would then be trapped in the net. With the advent of gunpowder, a slower dog was needed to make the birds rise to the gun and to pick up those which fell at a distance or to catch the runners. The gundog does not need to have speed, but it should have determination to press on through brambles and woodland, and be ready to enter water if necessary, even diving from a steep bank which other dogs are reluctant to do.

The gundog must be of steady temperament, not impetuous, and capable of remaining still in the face of temptation. They must not be possessive, so will not have much guard instinct, but they are also not noisy. Above all, the gundog is willing and keen, alert and interested in all that goes on, tolerant of other dogs and responsive to commands of people other than its owner. Given all these desirable qualities it is obvious that the gundog will make an excellent companion, but it is essential that if the dog is not worked or entered in obedience trials, some interesting exercise is provided. The dog may be played with in an appropriate way, fetching and carrying and 'hide and seek' all stretch the dogs considerable natural talent.

The gundog must have a 'soft' mouth and be capable of carrying an object without crushing or harming it, which makes it gentle with children. The dog should not be allowed to snatch or to tug a toy; teach your dog to 'give' or 'drop it' and it should instantly comply.

The setters, English, Irish and Gordon (Scottish) are the largest gundogs, and were probably among the earliest used. They are all big dogs requiring ample room indoors and out. It is unkind to blame a setter for sweeping all the china from a table with its plumed tail if it hardly has room to turn round. The Irish or Red Setter has a typically volatile, gay temperament, and remains puppylike for a long time.

This dog is best suited to life in the country and a big garden. The English Setter, with coloured tickings on a white base, is a little heavier in build and steadier in behaviour. The Gordon is black with tan trimmings, bred in this colouring by the Dukes of Newcastle to be less conspicuous on moorland. A heavier dog again, some authorities say, there is Bloodhound in its make-up. The setters need careful rearing, restricted exercise up to six months and then only gentle walking until they are a year old.

Right
The colouring of this English Setter is known as orange Belton, the name coming from a Northumberland village near the home of a pioneer of the breed. There are also blue and lemon Beltons. Most English Setter puppies are born white, the flecked markings starting to appear when the pups are three weeks old.

Below
This Irish Setter puppy is about nine weeks old, beautifully reared with strong bone in the forelegs and clean, dark eyes. The trusting, steady gaze indicates a puppy well conditioned to household surroundings, unafraid of humans and ready to learn to be a sensible companion.

The wise and sensible Gordon Setter is the heaviest of the setters. The dog pictured has very well-laid shoulders, giving great galloping stamina and a far-reaching stride. The coat is mainly black with tan eyebrows, muzzle, throat and inside of the legs and the plumed tail hangs gracefully.

The pointers were developed for precision work by the shooting man, around the turn of the twentieth century. There are several pointer varieties, all of which originated in Europe, where game has always been scarce and so important to locate. Pointers hunt by scent keeping their heads high. In the point they are rigid, head in the direction of the birds, tail extended and foot raised, until given the command to flush the birds for the guns. These dogs are much used in stubble and open country by lone guns who like to be discriminating about their bag. Pointers are country dogs and should be kept where exercise and sport are available.

The Weimaraner, in distinctive pearl grey coat, was once the guard and gundog of the nobles of the Weimar Republic in Germany. The smooth coat of silver or lavender grey is no problem to care for. Some people are not attracted by the yellow eyes which occasionally have an unexpectedly hostile expression. Choose a Weimaraner from parents of good temperament, and instil discipline from puppy days, as this is probably the least mild of the gundogs. The Vizsla, a Hungarian gundog, is a dog of similar type said to be capable of all work in the shooting field. It is an intelligent dog which deserves to have work to do and should not be kept idle.

Having shot his birds the sportsman is not happy until they are in his bag, whole and undamaged, so he needs a retrieving dog. They are essentially animals which like carrying things; dogs which will jump into icy water and pick up a live bird without mangling it or wanting to eat it. The St John's dogs or the smaller varieties of Newfoundland, used by fishermen to pick up fish, haul nets and carry messages from ship to shore, proved suitable as a base for the development of the retriever. The Flatcoat Retriever evolved from a setter and Newfoundland cross. Not a very striking dog in appearance, it excels in willingness and loyalty to its owner, and is very easy to train.

Above
On point, this efficient English Pointer is indicating with every line of its body the presence of birds in the stubble. The head is a fine example of the breed, having the dished face, defined stop and forward-looking eye the judges look for. The colours are liver, black or lemon on white.

Left
The Great Münsterländer, a tall white and black dog, comes from Germany. A strong and active hunter, the dog's outline indicates its strength and speed. There is light feathering on the ears, legs and low-carried tail. The jaw is long and powerful, and great attention would be paid to tooth placement in the show ring.

Right
These German Short-haired Pointers have an attractive ticked coat, but solid colours are also permitted. The head has less stop than the English Pointer. The eyes are set obliquely and have a somewhat sharp expression, although light yellow eyes are penalized in the show ring. The dogs in the picture show the correct, long, sloping shoulder.

Above
The Hungarian Vizsla is smooth-coated, a rusty gold shade with eyes and nose to match. The skull is wide between the ears, and the nose has wide-open nostrils to admit scent. The neck is muscular, well set on the shoulders of the strong body with well-rounded ribs. These dogs carry no excess weight and are capable of maximum activity.

The Chesapeake Bay Retriever is a native American breed, kept in large numbers in USA as a hunting companion, but little seen in Britain. A big dog with a waterproof coat in a variety of shades, the short hair is in ripple-like waves on the shoulders, back and neck. The dog's fondness for water makes it an excellent aid for the wildfowler.

The Labrador Retriever is the big dog that can be anything man asks of it. Genial, aimiable, patient with children, reliable as a blind person's guide, the Labrador can be trained to do anything but attack. As a bored pet, it settles in to middle age very quickly, and may then become dull, greedy, overweight and lethargic. The Labrador needs plenty of exercise and constructive play, for it is a pity to waste this dog's endless talents. The naturally dull-surfaced double coat tends to shed more or less all the year round if the dog is kept in a warm environment.

The Golden Retriever is another powerfully built 'carrying' dog, a little bulkier than the Labrador, with a feathery wavy coat of gold or cream, which requires regular grooming. Their temperament is very good and Goldens are cheerful, if somewhat clumsy as puppies. With their many talents, it should always be possible for children to devise a game in which the Goldie can take part. Labradors, Golden Retrievers and spaniels have a tendency to a deformity of the hip joint known as hip dysplasia (HD) and also have hereditary eye defects. The breeder selling a puppy should know to what degree the parents are affected. In many cases a dog which is shown on an X-ray to be affected with HD may never be seriously incommoded. HD can only be assessed by X-ray at about eighteen months. Some of the eye defects do not manifest themselves until the dog is middle aged, and very often the owner will not suspect blindness, as the dog can manage well by scenting power in familiar places. A wrong positioning of eyelashes, growing inwards or outwards or in double rows, is common in many gundog and working breeds and may cause irritation and discharge from the eye. The condition can be corrected surgically, but affected dogs must not be bred from, as the malformation may be passed to future generations.

Left
This Weimaraner bitch and her puppy show the very beautiful mauve-grey coat which attracts so many people to the breed. The longish ears are set high on the aristocratic head. The pale yellow eyes can have an arrogant expression even when the dog is friendly, although these gundogs have definite guarding instincts.

Right
The Chesapeake Bay Retriever is an eager and strong working dog. The coat, which is curly on the back and smoother on legs and flanks, is always a shade of brown. The Chesapeake has very active oil glands in the coat, very necessary for a water dog but making it give off a somewhat disagreeable odour in the house.

Left
At one time yellow Labradors were almost discarded, but lately they have become very popular as pets, although the blacks are still regarded as superior for working ability. The ears on the dogs in the picture are small and hang correctly close to the head, and the necks are strong and muscular to enable the dogs to lift heavy birds.

Above
This Golden Retriever has the benevolent look so typical of this breed. A wide range of cream to golden shades is permitted by the breed standards. When choosing a puppy remember that the coat darkens as the dog becomes adult. This dog has fine shoulders, a level back, powerful hind quarters with well turned stifles and a correctly set tail.

The Cocker Spaniel (known as the English Cocker in USA) derives its name either from the pursuit of woodcock or the Elizabethan word 'cockering' meaning an expression of affection in excess. Either word aptly describes these spaniels which were the most popular of sporting and companion dogs for many years. Like all breeds that have reached the top rank of demand from the public, the Cocker has had to pay the price in indiscriminate breeding and generations of unemployment which have spoilt the temperament to some extent, especially in the reds and goldens. The Cocker is required to be merry and fearless, an extrovert willing to join in any family activity. A sullen, fat dog, drawing back from the extended hand, or excited to the point of hysteria is the type to be avoided.

The Welsh Springer Spaniel, originally used for springing game into the net, is larger than the Cocker, rich red and white in coat, and has so far missed being exploited by popularity. The Welsh Springer looks to be built for work, which it thoroughly enjoys, and is not a dog to sit idle in an enclosed room. The English Springer Spaniel is a larger dog again, weighing up to 50 pounds (22 kilograms), twice the weight of a Cocker. These keen workers would be unhappy in a town home.

Right
The Sussex Spaniel's glowing, golden-brown coat is a distinguishing feature of this heavy dog with the eyes and nose brown to tone. The coat darkens several shades if the dog lives in warm conditions indoors. The body is long and the dog moves with a characteristic rolling gait.

Below
The Clumber Spaniel takes its name from the seat of the Dukes of Newcastle at Clumber Park. A massive dog, it is not as demonstrative as other spaniels, being rather slow and ponderous in its attitude to life. The dog here shows the heavy bone, thick neck, straight and powerful back and lightly marked white coat demanded in the breed standard.

The Field Spaniel is a variety somewhat in decline, not having the glamour of the Cocker or the distinction of the Springer. The Field Spaniel is an excellent worker of docile temperament, well suited to obedience or gun training.

The Cocker (USA), known as the American Cocker in Britain, is descended from British dogs, but how they changed while crossing the Atlantic! In USA the breed developed a rounded skull, shorter nose, longer neck and sloping topline. Enormous length of feathering is valued, ears are twice the depth of the head, and the whole space between front and back legs is filled with a long fall of hair. This coat will require professional clipper stripping on the head and skilled thinning with scissors on the body about every two months. An American Cocker in show coat could not be allowed loose in brambles and bracken for fear of tearing the coat. The American Cocker is now on probation with the British Kennel Club to retain its grouping with the gundogs, but several individual dogs have proved they have all the right instincts for work.

The Sussex Spaniel is a heavy, low-moving animal with a trace of Bloodhound in its expression. Long-bodied and low slung, the Sussex has a unique rolling gait and it gives tongue, when hunting, as a hound does. Plenty of outdoor exercise is necessary for this breed. Persevering in cover, the Sussex makes a good roughshooter's dog, but does not suit hunting conditions in America.

The Clumber is the heaviest of the spaniels, a slow, deliberate hunter, rather dignified and closely resembling its ancestors owned by the Dukes of Newcastle before 1800. As with all dogs of massive bone, the Clumber needs care in early rearing, with exercise only in relation to the pup's ability.

The American Water Spaniel is a breed native to the mid-west of America, and there is none registered with the British Kennel Club. Medium-sized, with liver or chocolate coat waved on the back, curly on chest and ears, the appearance is not very striking, but their working ability is second to none. The Irish Water Spaniel is also brown, but has attractive curls all over the body, and hanging ringlets on the ears. This tall dog is keen and steady at work and playful in the home. The coat does not moult, but needs combing through, and the dog should also have the opportunity to swim, to keep the coat in the correct tight curl.

The Brittany Spaniel, of French origin, is common in America but the breed is not yet recognized in Britain. In size it is between spaniel and setter. The Brittany is the only spaniel to point game. A leggy dog with smooth ears and only a little feathering, this breed is naturally tailless, or short docked.

This American Cocker Spaniel (the Cocker in USA) shows the fully chiselled head with definite stop, the broad and deep muzzle, and low set ears with very long feathering. The body is short and compact. The enormous length of coat is valued in the show ring, and a wide variety of colours are permitted.

Left
The Field Spaniel derives from the larger type of Cocker. It has become a well-balanced dog built for stamina and endurance without exaggerated features. The muzzle is long to allow for great scenting ability. The Field Spaniel should be solid colour, and white markings are a show fault.

Below
This tall dog shows the beautiful orange and white coat colour of the Brittany Spaniel, and also the long thrusting neck peculiar to the breed. The eyes are amber and the nose brownish. The silky coat is lightly feathered compared to the other spaniels and the tail is naturally short.

Right
The Irish Water Spaniel always looks as though it can't do a thing with its hair, but the crisp, harsh coat, which does not moult, is ideal for a dog which works in and out of water, needing only a shake to dry. The face, front of neck, hind legs and most of the tail are naturally smooth and without curls.

Working dogs

The working dogs have three types of duty – as guard dogs, transport or draught dogs and stockherders. At one time, when roads were narrow, and paths steep and hilly, it was common to use large and heavy shouldered dogs to pull small carts, and carry light loads in panniers, but abuse of the dogs has led to this work being forbidden by law in Britain. In the Arctic regions, communities could hardly survive without sled dogs, and pulling or carrying is well within the capacity of many large breeds. All dogs classified by the Kennel Club in the working group are regarded as being fit for some work, although many thousands have no job beyond supervising their owner's property which they do by instinct, without special instruction. For this reason, all dogs in the working group must be treated with respect and some caution; they should not be teased and their warnings must be taken seriously, for when they say 'No', they mean 'No', as any intruder, or even friendly caller will find out. The guard dog does not have a fierce demeanour all the time and usually they are most genial. They must never be under-estimated, however, as their protective instinct can rise in seconds, sometimes with only a change in the expression of the eyes to indicate that someone has gone too far.

The owner of a working dog must be aware of the necessity to control the animal from puppy days; a guard dog must be obedient to its owner, otherwise it is downright dangerous. The working dog has respect for a pack leader and a need to be dominated, firmly but kindly and with sympathy. Every command given to a working dog must be followed up until it is obeyed, so that the dog never experiences the heady pleasure of defiance, which can so easily become a habit. The working dog must come when called, infallibly, and must give up any prize easily. It is also important to be able to stop the dog when it is running at speed. In general, these dogs were bred to work closely with man and their instinct is to stay close to home and to watch everything that happens so they will not be inclined to wander.

Right
This splendid Old English Sheepdog stands in the type of pasture where it can be of immense help to the shepherd in gathering sheep to one area, separating a few, or rounding up the back of the flock when the shepherd moves them to a new field. For the show ring, the coat should be very full, the hair falling over the eyes. The hair colour is grey or blue with white markings.

Above
The Smooth Collie and the Rough
Collie are alike in body and head
shape, only the length of coat being
different. The heads are long, tapering
to a point, with almond-shaped eyes.
The ears stand erect, with just the tip
falling forward. These dogs are
tricolours, with dark eyes. The blue
merle is an alternative colouring.

Most guard breeds are wonderful with children, moderating a natural inclination for roughness to the size of their playmates. Guard dogs should not be left with a group of young children and should not be taken out by them, in case some situation arises which the dog interprets as danger; few children could hold a guarding dog as, with the exception of the Corgi, all the workers are quite large. These big dogs must never pull on the lead, or they turn their owner into a comic sight, whereas a huge dog walking close on a slack lead is a compliment to dog and owner. Guard dogs should not walk to heel, but at their owner's side. This group needs careful rearing, with controlled exercise during the growing period. A large bed on which to stretch full length is a necessity, and plenty of padding should be provided to avoid ugly joint callouses on heavy dogs. In all the large breeds, bitches are distinctly smaller, lighter and more biddable than the males, but the females are even more devoted and courageous as personal guards in time of necessity.

The Mastiff is one of the most ancient of dogs, probably introduced into Britain by Phoenician traders before the first Roman invasion. Similar dogs are found all over Europe, descending from the Molossus which travelled with the Roman armies, doing all sorts of work and also providing sport in contests against lions. The broad muzzle characterizes the fighting dog, and some Mastiff blood is found in all the heavy, guarding breeds. Scenting powers are not high in the Mastiff, and the dog is not long-sighted, but very observant of the slightest move made at short range. A huge dog to feed, the Mastiff really needs specialist rearing, as they are a late maturing breed. Although the breed had almost died out in Britain after World War II, many good specimens had been sent to USA for safe keeping, so allowing a postwar revival by fanciers in both countries.

The Bull Mastiff is a deliberate Bulldog and Mastiff cross. Known as the gamekeeper's night dog, it fulfils this role as a quiet, fearless animal which will catch and hold an intruder, but not inflict further injury. In the home, they are loving and cheerful, needing some formal exercise everyday, as they tend to be lazy if left to their own devices. Weighing some 130 pounds (58·5 kilograms), the Bull Mastiff is powerful, but gentle with children. It is not a very long-lived dog, eight or nine years being average.

This team of Siberian dogs is in working harness, pulling a light load at moderate speed across firm snow. For racing, the dogs would be harnessed further apart, and if they were working over treacherous sea ice or crevasses, the dogs would be on long, individual traces fanning out from a central point, to allow any dog to save itself should it fall through the ice. The harnesses sit low on the shoulder and around the chest. Dogs do not pull from a neck collar, because pressure at the carotid artery can cause a blood deficiency to the brain, tending to make the dog's natural reflexes less acute.

The Boxer is the Mastiff descendant which has made good, not in public employment, but as the popular companion guard dog in the home, being of a size to command respect but not too large to feed and exercise. The breed emerged in Germany at the end of last century, owing something to the German Bullenbeisser, and also to the old tall type of English Bulldog. The ponderance and heaviness of the Molossus is missing, from the spare, well-muscled frame of the Boxer which has great power in the shoulder, a strong square bite, and an enormous comprehension of human thought which goes beyond intelligence. With the good qualities goes obstinacy, love of comfort, and an enormous sense of humour which tends at times to override discipline. Boxers, mostly brindle, more square and squat than the present show standard, served with the armies in the Middle East in World War II as silent and ever-alert guards for airfields. The biggest snag about the Boxer as a companion dog is that they are very dependent on human company, and are often claustrophobic if left alone, taking out their frustrations by damaging their surroundings, so the Boxer should never be kept by people who expect to be away from home a lot. A wonderful dog with children,

the Boxer will enjoy play right into old age. Ten years is the average lifespan.

The Rottweiler is a strong dog of Roman origin, bred as a guard and cattle dog in the German town of Rottweil. Weighing some 130 pounds (58·5 kilograms), the Rott must be controlled by force of personality, when it becomes the most dignified and reserved of guards, never treacherous with its owners and their children. Early firm training will pay dividends, as this dog has an endless capacity for learning.

The Dobermann Pinscher is a 'stripped down for action' dog built on racehorse lines. A custom-made dog, it is the epitome of all that the Germans expect from a guard and police dog. This breed was the deliberate creation of one Herr Dobermann, the dog catcher of the town of Apolda, who used the best Pinschers, Danes, German Shepherds, Schnauzers, Rottweilers and Black and Tan Terriers in a planned breeding programme to produce the ultimate in working dogs – alert, sharp and intelligent, with great purity of form. The Dobermann gives loyalty to one owner, and needs firm control always, but is capable of being extremely devoted to a sensible family.

Below
This Cardiganshire Welsh Corgi shows with pride its full tail which is never docked. The expressive ears are held high, and the body is long and low to the ground, on short legs.

Bottom
This Newfoundland is taking part in the water trials held every year in order to perpetuate the breed's natural ability for swimming and lifesaving. The dog is held close to the boat while a swimmer plunges into the lake. The dog then attempts to rescue the 'drowning' man, usually with great success.

These Alsatians or German Shepherd Dogs are enjoying the kind of exercise which is essential to this intelligent and strong dog, which cannot use its powers to the full being walked on a lead around the streets. The dog on the left is clearing the stile in the manner necessary for field trial competitions, where dogs are tested for agility, obedience and courage.

The Great Dane is another descendant of the Mastiff, probably with some Greyhound blood. The breed has little connection with Denmark, being kept mostly in central Europe for hunting boar. A most amiable dog in the home, but with a height of 36 inches (0·9 metres) at the shoulder in the male, it can reach most of your shelves when it stands upright, and it needs considerable space to lie down. The Dane is a deterrent by reason of size and deep resonant bark, but the breed is not at all fierce, and they are immediately friendly with callers. Not an easy breed to rear well, the Dane is not greedy and sometimes will not take as much food as is necessary to make the growth expected in youth. This is a magnificent dog, more easily controlled than some of the smaller guarding breeds.

The Saint Bernard owes a lot to Roman Molossus blood, and also to interbreeding with the Pyrenean Mountain Dog and Newfoundland, by the monks of the St Bernard Hospice who required useful dogs to accompany them when they were called out to rescue travellers crossing the Alps on foot. The St Bernard's history is surrounded in legend, attaching to these dogs improbable stories of heroism and fortitude. A more accurate picture would be of a stalwart, tracking dog, which would 'down, stay' by a fallen traveller, giving comfort and body warmth; a dog big enough to carry a life-saving pack of food and blankets and also sturdy enough to make a path through deep snow which the traveller

could follow. The St Bernard's head gives an impression of benevolence which does not always echo the dog's true character. Children should not be allowed to exasperate these very large dogs, which can get uncomfortable in hot weather.

The Bernese Mountain Dog is another Mastiff type, rather shorter in the leg with powerful shoulders, which is ideally adapted for pulling small loads over mountain tracks in its native Switzerland. Provided the cart is well balanced and the load suited to their capabilities, the Mastiff-type dogs are well able to perform this work and seem to enjoy active employment on which they can accompany their master. The Bernese is recognized by the American Kennel Club and there are now a few of the breed in Britain.

The Pyrenean Mountain dog (Great Pyrenees) is another of the Molossus tribe, a dog of immense size with a thick white double coat. Being slow to mature, the Pyrenean needs control and careful rearing from puppy days. This is a dog which you need to buy from a specialist breeder, as following a win at the famous Cruft's Show many substandard Pyreneans were bred.

The Bouvier de Flandres is a Belgian working dog. Rough coated and broad in the muzzle, it is a very capable worker and war dog, although of unprepossessing appearance. The Bouvier is popular as a housedog in Europe, and is just becoming established in USA and Britain.

No one with sense would attempt to pass these two alert Dobermann Pinschers, on guard at the entrance to their owner's property. The dog on the right shows a fine, straight front and well-tucked-up loins, but she is flying her ears, which should be neatly folded to the head.

The Newfoundland is an all-weather dog, as much at home in water as on land, as its weatherproof coat and webbed feet show. The painter Landseer made the breed famous in Victorian times. Owing to the immense size and consequent need for large quantities of food there were very few in Britain at the end of World War II, and the breed would have died out but for the gift of a bitch in whelp from the American Newfoundland Club, which helped to restart the breed. The Newfie is an excellent dog with children, but a male of 150 pounds (67·5 kilograms) will have a huge coat to shed in summer, making a considerable amount of housework.

The Siberian Husky is an Arctic sled dog, capable of enduring very harsh conditions cheerfully. Many explorers have said how much they admired the courage and pride of these dogs, which seem to be able to bear anything but loss of status among the pack. The sled dog's instinct is to challenge for superiority, whether the pack leader is human or canine, so this breed must have firm control always. In America and Europe, husky-team racing is a thriving competitive sport.

The Alaskan Malamute is the heavy-freight carrier of the far north. Very intelligent and teachable dogs, they are very popular in USA, but there are only a few in Britain where it is difficult to provide the right conditions for these capable dogs.

These fawn Great Dane puppies are at an age when the breeder would say they should not be loooked at, as they are gawky adolescents. The heads do not yet have the nobility of the adult Dane. The lumpy joints in the legs are at the ends of the long bones where growth takes place, and they will not show when the dog is adult.

The great head of this Mastiff shows the desirable black mask over the muzzle, running up to include the eyes. The ears must be black too, with plenty of wrinkle on the head. The coat colour may be fawn or brindle, but the 'points' are always black.

The massive domed head of this St Bernard shows the typically benevolent expression associated with these great dogs. The eyes are small and deepset, showing a red rim (the haw). There are rough and smooth coats, the colouring being red or brown with white markings and black on face and ears.

45

The Samoyed is also from the Arctic, as its full white coat proclaims. This dog is very good as a companion to children, but the coat will require grooming, and a quantity of hair is shed at least twice a year.

Ever since man began keeping cattle, sheep and deer in herds, he had need of a dog to round up stragglers, keep beasts on the move, and to protect the herd from wolves or rustlers when encamped overnight. Two types of dog evolved – the nimble and clever herder, and the larger fierce animal, often whitecoated so that it showed up against the wolf. Many countries have their native sheepherding dogs, the British being the Collie, the Shetland Sheepdog (Sheltie), the Bearded Collie, Old English Sheepdog and the Pembroke and Cardigan Corgis.

The Rough Collie, sometimes wrongly called the Scotch Collie, is the best known, having been featured in many 'Lassie' films, but there is also a smooth variety which is less trouble when hair is shed. Collie temperament is good, although the dog should have companionship and an outdoor life to bring out its inborn intelligence.

The Shetland Sheepdog is very similar in appearance, but half the size, and rather more noisy. The Sheltie is a busy dog, quick moving and very trainable. Many work in obedience tests, but some under-exercised dogs tend to be excitable. The Sheltie is an adaptable pet for families which like a good walk at weekends.

The Old English Sheepdog was until quite recently a farm dog working with sheep and cattle. Advertising appeal has made this breed's popularity rocket, with consequent overbreeding and loss of temperament through these working dogs being kept in unsuitable environments. The enormous coat is intended for a dog living outside. In centrally heated homes the skin of the Old English will sometimes give trouble, and a dog confined too much will become destructive and irritable. Working dogs were often sheared with the sheep, and if the Bobtail is to be kept in full coat a lot of grooming is involved. Wire brushes should not be used, but the tangles teased out by hand, and the face washed after meals to prevent the dog getting unpleasant to be near.

Left
Here are Rough Collies with their smaller relations, the small sheepdog of the Shetland Isles, the Sheltie. The smaller dog is not an exact miniature of the large Collie, as there are several differences in the breed standards. The Sheltie on the right shows the closer ear placement which gives this breed a more alert expression than that of the Collie.

Below left
These Boxers have the alert and wary look characteristic of this guarding breed. British and American exhibitors prefer Boxers with white markings on the head and round the neck in a collar shape, leaving the black mask over the muzzle. However, the red bitches would be preferred by exhibitors in Europe where white is not liked.

Below
This Bull Mastiff shows the correct deep chest, powerful loins and straight front legs of a dog bred to be a guard to be reckoned with. The colour may be fawn or brindle with Mastiff-type black mask and dark eyes. This dog has a very good level topline. The tail is left undocked.

47

The Bearded Collie is not unlike a smaller version of the Old English, but with less coat and facial hair, and a long natural tail. This is a breed which enthusiasts admire because of the absence of artificial interference. The Beardie must have plenty of free exercise and a long walk each day. Brushing and regular baths are essential for a dog living in the house.

The Welsh Corgis, Pembrokeshire and Cardiganshire, are cattle dogs of great verve and ability. Although so small, they can control a bullock herd by nipping the hooves or gripping the noses if the cattle should be so misguided as to charge at the dog. They avoid being kicked by gripping the hoof, and swerving with the bullock, barking all the time. As a companion dog the Corgi shows energy, courage and tenacity. They are not very friendly and not easily caught when they do not wish to come to hand. The coat is shed twice a year, otherwise this breed does not demand a lot of grooming.

The Briard is the sheepdog of France, a tall dog with rough, shaggy coat, and hair falling over the eyes. The temperament is extrovert and cheerful, giving an energetic dog which makes an excellent family pet, as rising registration figures at both English and American Kennel Clubs indicate.

The Belgian Shepherd dogs are the Groenedael, Tervuren and Mallionois. Their appearance is much the same, except for the coat, the Groenendael being black, Tervueren red with black mask, and the Mallinois smooth-coated, fawn or red. All are fine outdoor workers, of excellent disposition.

The Alsatian or German Shepherd Dog is the greatest of the workers, being adaptable as war or police dog, guide for the blind, a guard dog or a companion. This is a breed which should be suspicious of strangers, not easily friendly but reliable and intensely loyal to its owners. The German Shepherd Dog bought from good stock, reared in plenty of space and decent surroundings has no superior as a family companion, although obedience to command is essential from puppy days, as an uncontrolled dog of such power is inevitably a danger. The overriding virtues of this breed are its intelligence and willingness to learn, and its devotion to a wise and firm owner. Admired and used the world over for its dignity and self-confidence, the German Shepherd Dog must never be goaded into aggression to bolster up it's owner's weakness.

Keen, alert and ready to obey its owner's bidding, the Bearded Collie makes a rewarding pet or working companion. The long hair falls over the head, but does not entirely obscure the bright eyes. Colour is grey, fawn, black or brown with white markings, and the standard requires dark eyes and nose.

Right
Alert and eager for work or play, the Alaskan Malamute is capable of great endurance, and the strong shoulders have enormous pulling power. The coat colour may be in all shades of grey while the face markings and ear linings are cream. The small, pricked ears are a feature of the breed.

Below
Like most of the animals of the Arctic circle, the Samoyed is camouflaged in white, but eyes, lip rims and nose are jet black. The tail is lightly curled over the back, and the feet are long and flat to enable the dog to run for long distances pulling a load. The deep chest and rounded body give great working capacity.

The Briard is a French sheepdog which in its native land would have cropped ears from which the hair would droop, in elegant cascades. This British bred example has natural ears and hair covering the eyes which normally have a bright and mischievous expression. The coat, although long, is easy to keep clean.

The Puli, Kuvasz and Komondor are the sheepherding dogs of the Hungarian plains. The Puli is an active, vocal herder, extremely nimble and alert. This breed has lately been taken up in Britain, the attraction lying in the unique corded formation of the very profuse coat. The Puli does not need clipping or very formal grooming, but the cords must be torn up and divided from time to time. Owners say this is a soothing occupation to be done while watching television. In America, the Puli coat is combed out, in something resembling poodle style, but purists feel that this is not typical of the Puli.

The Komondor is a very large, Mastiff-sized dog, also covered in long shaggy hair, which will become corded. To keep this dog in 'house' condition will mean a very big grooming task, as in their native land the Komondor was accustomed to live out in all weathers. These dogs are said to be passive in the day, and become active at night, as their ancient duties were to guard the flock while the shepherd rested. The Komondor is a very keen guard, and probably not a dog the average family would find easy to own.

The Kuvasz is of medium size with a more normal type of white coat which forms a ruff round the neck. It is not unlike the Pyrenean Mountain Dog and the Maremma. A hard worker and agreeable companion, this dog must live in the country and have hard exercise. All the Hungarian dogs are said to do well on the plainest of diets, as they were never indulged in their working state, and lived outdoors in the hardest conditions.

Above
The Kuvasz is a large, gracefully built Hungarian working dog, with a double white coat which must have no curl. Eyes, nose and lips must be dark and the expression should be kindly. Although heavy, the Kuvasz can move at great speed, and shows courage and intelligence as a working or household companion.

Right
The Komondor is a Hungarian dog, formerly used as a guard for the nomadic flocks of sheep. This large dog is totally covered with a white coat, of coarse texture on the outside covering a woolly undercoat, the whole naturally forming cords and tassels, a coat form only found on this breed and on the Puli.

Left
The Bernese Mountain Dog comes from Switzerland, where its work is to pull small carts over mountain tracks. Small traders use these dogs to deliver household supplies. The coat is soft and smooth, the white blaze on the head and the white chest being required by the breed standard, as well as the bright tan above the eyes and on the legs.

Above
The Bouvier de Flandres is covered with long, shaggy hair. In his homeland of Belgium and other Continental countries, the ears are cropped, adding to the fierce expression of this dog whose anger is not to be trifled with, although it is very loyal and equable with its owners.

Right
The Gronendael is a long-haired dog, black in colour. The body hair is long and sleek, contrasting with the ruff or mane around the chest. The tail is long and plumed. Although the body is narrow, the chest should be deep, with the back topline sloping easily down to the croup. The triangular ears are naturally erect.

53

Terriers

Sharp is the word for terriers; audacity, courage and perseverance are other adjectives which aptly describe these keen dogs of which there are many regional varieties in Britain. The name terrier derives from the latin *terra* meaning earth, both because this is a dog which will go to ground, and because these were the dogs of the peasants, the hounds and spaniels being the prerogative of the nobility. From early times the terriers had a 'cloth cap' image, but this is being reversed, for now a smartly trimmed pedigreed terrier has a very exclusive image. Terriers must be lively, inquisitive and quick. In the farmyard they are tireless ratters, about the house they keep busy and to a great extent exercise themselves just by minding everyone's affairs. Game and aggressive against their natural prey, they can also, if not mastered, be a little quick on the snap with humans. Most terriers are already convinced of their own self-importance, so it is imperative that from puppy days they are taught their place in the social scale, kindly but firmly.

Terrier coats, with a few exceptions, need a fair amount of grooming, so puppies should be accustomed to being stood on a table for coat grooming, whisker trimming and other necessary attentions from the time they go to their new homes. One of the reasons for the decline in terriers as pets is that many varieties need stripping right out twice a year, if the pup you buy is to look anything like those shown in the beauty ring. In order to keep coat texture correct, the stripping should be hand done, pulling out the hair gradually with thumb and forefinger, a time consuming process for which professional handstrippers are rightly well paid. Clippers can be used on the pet dog, in the same manner as for Poodles, but the result is nothing approaching the classic terrier trim. Also, cutting or clipping the coat leaves the roots still in the skin, causing irritation, and clogging the growth of new hair, so it is well worth learning to remove dead hair manually. Terriers were at one time thought to be prone to skin troubles, but thorough grooming promotes blood circulation and does a lot to keep the skin healthy. Harsh-coated dogs should not be bathed often, as soap softens the coat and makes it take up dirt more quickly.

Most terriers are good and trustworthy with children, they are certainly always ready to join in any activity, if a trifle noisily. The tendency to snap the jaws quickly, so desirable in a good vermin killer, may cause some frights to tiny children, but terriers, like other breeds, can be trained to give and take gently. These hardy dogs are not fussy feeders, and are not difficult to rear. Due to their unexaggerated physical conformation, terriers do not suffer with many skeletal abnormalities. Exercise can be as flexible as the owner wishes, as terriers are among the few dogs which keep active on their own, and they have a reasonable measure of independence.

The 'king of terriers', the Airedale, is the only terrier to be used as a police and war dog in Britain. Bred to hunt otter on the banks of the River Aire in the Midlands, the Airedale is still fearless in water, and a great companion and working dog. A professional trim makes all the difference to its smart outline.

The Welsh Terrier resembles a small Airedale, weighing some 20 pounds (9 kilograms) against the Airedale's 50 pounds (22 kilograms). The colouring, black

These delightful Wire Fox Terrier puppies are between three and four months old and are just cutting their adult teeth. They still have their fluffy baby coats but will soon require their first formal stripping into angular terrier style.

Above
This West Highland White (Westie) puppy already shows all the character of the breed, the gay mischievous outlook on life, and the pure white coat with dark eyes and black nose. The forelegs are well developed for digging, and the strong jaws capable of killing vermin. The body is strongly built, shoulders slope back and the hindquarters are well muscled.

Left
This smooth Fox Terrier head illustrates perfectly the eager temperament so valued in the breed. The V-shaped ears are in line with the corner of the small eyes, which have the characteristic, penetrating stare. The long foreface gives power to the jaws, while the muscular neck allows the head the mobility which a keen ratter needs.

and tan, is the same and the coat is harsh and wiry. This handy little terrier has great character, but must not be allowed to get out of hand. The correct chiselled appearance can only be obtained by regular trimming.

The Lakeland Terrier, smaller again, is very game indeed, having originally been bred to go to ground and kill foxes in sheep-farming country. The Lakeland has supreme courage and tenacity, but in the home makes a great companion dog.

Several varieties of short-legged terriers originate from Scotland, where they worked foxes gone to ground in masses of granite boulders, their short legs making it possible to dig in rock-hard earth. In times when travel was difficult, and there was little need to move about the country, these terriers were isolated in the areas after which they were named. The Scottish Terrier itself is very typical, with long head, harsh coat and strong whiskery jaws. It is often called a Scottie, but the name Aberdeen terrier should not be used.

The Cairn and the West Highland White (Westie) were regarded as the same breed until 1925. They come from the West Highlands and Hebrides, where at one time only the darker coated puppies were kept, the white dogs being too noticeable for the gamekeeper. When the breed was taken up by exhibitors, white puppies were kept and shown, and to save confusion, the two colours were separated. The gay and gallant character of these dogs makes them very popular in the home. Both breeds need expert trimming twice a year.

The Skye Terrier is closely related to the Cairn, but is distinguished by the long fall of hair which comes from a centre parting running from head to tail, with softer feathering on the ears. All dogs with these hair-covered faces must have a face wash after meals. The Skye is decidedly suspicious of strangers, even actively unfriendly, but is devoted to its owner. This dog is probably most successful with an adult family.

The Manchester Terrier is elegant and urbane in smooth black and tan coat. This dog shows well the sloping shoulders and strong hindquarters required by the breed standard. The tucked-up loins assist the dog in making a quick turn in a small space. The correct areas for the tan markings are clearly shown.

Left
The Soft-coated Wheaten Terrier from Ireland is shown in its natural untrimmed state, with soft honey-coloured coat covering the whole body and hanging over the eyes, which should be dark, and the nose black. An energetic, sound dog, full of fun and activity, the Wheaten deserves greater popularity.

Bottom left
The Cairn Terrier must have a rugged highland appearance, with a double untrimmed coat, not carved into an artificially fashionable outline. The coat may be tidied up by plucking, and for health reasons excess hair should be removed from inside the ears, between the feet and on the tail.

Above
The Welsh Terrier is near in size to the wire-haired Fox Terrier, but less finely built. The puppies are born black, but gradually the tan head, chest and leg furnishings appear so that at three months the pup has the adult colouring. In America, a smaller size is preferred to those shown in Britain.

Right
The Bedlington Terrier has a pear-shaped head, with a silky topknot. set on a long neck. The Bedlington is the only terrier to show the roached back in the manner of the Whippet type of dog. The dogs in the picture show the requisite long hare-feet of a dog which should move very fast.

The Sealyham comes from Wales, where it was a pack dog, used for ratting and badger digging. Thorough grooming is important for this breed, and professional trimming to get the sculptured look which owners find so attractive. Any overgrowth of hair inside the ears must be removed, as clogged ear channels are responsible for many ear troubles.

The terriers of Ireland include the Irish, which is like the Airedale in outline, but smaller and with a glorious red coat. It is a courageous dog which likes a scrap but loves its owners. The Kerry Blue is again a true terrier shape but with a short grey–blue coat, which usually only shows its true colour when the dog is adult. The Soft-coated Wheaten Terrier is a natural dog, shown without stripping or trimming. The Wheaten's coat does not shed hair and the breed is said to have inborn good sense and an ability to listen to orders, which many terriers lack. The Wheaten is likely to increase in popularity, although there are not yet enough representatives in America for it to be recognized by the American Kennel Club.

The Dandie Dinmonts from Northumberland are long, low-slung dogs with unique silky topknots of hair. The two colours in which they occur are known as mustard, (fawn to gold) and pepper (grey to black). A splendid, easily kept little dog, it is closely related to the Border Terrier, which is a little higher on the leg, shorter in body and without the top knot. Some Borders now being shown are quite compact and cobby. This is essentially a working terrier, a great companion for children, good ratters even in water, but well-behaved and undemonstrative in the house. Chasers of cats and small livestock, the Border Terrier must be trained from early days.

The Bedlington, which also comes from Northumberland, is quite distinct from the other terriers in having a soft lamb-like coat in liver or blue which appears in correct colour when the puppies are about three months old. The Bedlington outline is like that of a Whippet, giving speed and grace together with terrier attack. Hair is not shed, but grooming and trimming are essential. Bedlingtons are inclined to fight, especially if under-exercised and bored with too much confinement.

Left
The Scottie may be wheaten or brindle, although most people think of the breed as only in black. The head is long, set on a muscular neck and long, sloping shoulders. The ears must be pointed and erect. Correct trimming helps fill the desired block outline, with sharply up-pointing tail.

Above
'One false move and we'll be down', these Irish Terriers seem to say, fulfilling completely their breed standard which requires them to be alert, quick and keen, their character expressed in their eyes and ear carriage. The wiry coat is red or gold, with black nose and dark eyes.

The Airedale Terrier has only one colouring, tan with a black or grizzle saddle. The head is brick-shaped, the body short and well ribbed, and the front legs are absolutely straight. The V-shaped ears are set to the side of the skull giving the 'king of terriers' its characteristic jaunty air.

The Fox Terriers, wire-haired and smooth-haired, are among the smartest and hardiest of Britain's dogs, valued the world over for their vitality and sporting instincts. Their original purpose was to bolt the fox when hounds had driven it to ground, and the little terrier would be carried by the huntsman on the back of his horse, to be put down when needed.

The Norfolk and the Norwich Terriers were one breed as recently as 1964, when the drop-eared variety of Norwich was separated to become the Norfolk. Very game, energetic little dogs, they want only minimal coat tidying, and are adaptable for exercise, getting quite a lot from hunting around in a large garden. Like most terriers they are good with children, but they do not possess endless patience, so will not stand for being teased or roughly handled. In America, only the Norwich is recognized, with prick or drop ears being allowed.

The Manchester Terrier is black and tan, smooth coated, alert and bright-eyed, with beautiful, neat ear carriage. Not very friendly with strangers, these terriers may be just a bit too snappy for children unless they have always been used to a mixed age group in the family. Manchesters are almost professional rat killers and cat chasers, and may prove a little too noisy for town houses.

The Bull Terrier and related Staffordshire Bull Terrier are completely different from the badger and rodent terriers. These Bulldog and terrier crosses were bred for the spectator sports of bull- and bear-baiting and dog fighting, so courage and stamina were encouraged by selection. Both breeds have a lot of original Bulldog toughness, yet are very affectionate to their owners and very playful with children, but being such powerful dogs, still not averse to a scrap, they cannot be exercised by children alone. Determination is a keynote of Bull Terrier character. The intelligence of these Bulldog crosses is very high, so they need the stimulation of companionship and things happening around them to occupy their minds, or they will be destructive. All the Bull breeds tend to be claustrophobic, and cannot bear to be shut up alone, so they come to be good dogs to have on public premises like hotels, shops and bars where there is plenty going on and something to guard. For the right owners, the Bull Terrier and the hard-packed, cobbier Staffordshire make wonderful companions.

Above

Anybody want a fight? The Staffordshire Bull Terrier never lets the opportunity pass, yet in the home it is playful, affectionate and a great companion. The head is broader than that of the Bull Terrier, the foreface shorter, and the mouth opening is exceptionally wide, allowing a strong grip on an adversary. The barrel body is packed with hard muscle, and the feet turn out a little, allowing flexibility when fighting.

Left

The Bull Terrier has a unique head shape, very down-faced with extremely strong jaws giving an invincible grip. The neck is long and arched, the body barrel-shaped, packing weight and substance into every inch of the dog's frame. There are no size or weight limits in the breed standard.

Right and below
The young Norfolk Terrier is enjoying its native windswept beach, while the adult Norwich Terriers are equally at home in a well-kept garden. It can be seen that there are few differences in the breeds, beyond the drop- and pricked-ear carriage. Both types have terrific energy and will participate in any family activity. The body shape is stocky and the adults carry a full ruff of coat around the neck, the colouring being shades of red and black and tan.

The Skye Terrier is long and low, with a perfectly level back from which the hair cascades from a centre parting to cover the flanks right down to the ground. Ears can be drop or prick, the latter being most common. The ears are carried high with a falling fringe of dark hair.

Left
This is a pepper-coloured Dandie Dinmont, the other colour choice being the fawn to golden mustard. The body is long and flexible, to enable the dog to work well underground. The large domed head is covered with a white silky topknot, and the jaw is unusually powerful with strong teeth.

Left
The French Bulldog is a compact, well-balanced animal with broad, flat skull and huge, upright ears. Exaggerated features have been discouraged by breeders so that the Frenchie remains active and agile. These little dogs are affectionate and full of fun, but perhaps a little possessive about their owners. The two in the picture are dark brindles; black is not a favoured colour.

Below
The black or liver-coloured spots on the Dalmatian should be round and well separated, none bigger than a ten-pence piece. Puppies are white at birth, the spots gradually coming through at weaning time, as can be seen on the pups here. Ideally, even the long tail should have its quota of spots.

Utility dogs

The dogs which find themselves in the utility or miscellaneous group are the unemployed – those dogs which once had a job to do but find that fashion, or twentieth-century conditions have made them redundant, but which are still wanted as companion and house dogs. The Dalmatian is a good example. A dog with splendid conformation, capable of trotting smartly for many miles, the Dalmatian was in great demand to accompany carriages and dog carts, as guards and also gundogs. Now the elegance of the spotted dog is appreciated in a companion, as this dog expands in intelligence the more it has of human company. The Dally will not be destructive if given plenty of hard exercise. The breed is beset by hereditary deafness, often the plague of white-coated breeds, and Dalmatians also have a propensity to form kidney stones. A puppy's hearing can be tested at six weeks, and this should be done for all Dalmatians as deaf puppies appear in litters from two sound parents. The deaf puppy has no future at all and must be destroyed. In USA the Dalmatian is more constructively used, many being trained in obedience work and taking part in coaching and driving trials.

The present day Bulldog is a long way removed from the type of the butcher's dog popular at its heyday in 1800. The heavy, almost noseless dog we see in the show ring today would be hard put to it to have the breath to attack and hold on to a bull. The courage and spirit is there, but fashion has altered the animal's physical capability. Our modern Bull Terriers and Boxers are more like the original Bulldog. The Bully still has all the charm and sense of humour for which it is valued in many homes. Not an easy breed to whelp, owing to its shape, Bulldog puppies will always be expensive, and they are not long-lived dogs.

Whelping troubles also beset the French Bulldog, of the attractive, inquisitive face and huge upright 'bat' ears. The Frenchie is of more conventional dog shape than the English Bulldog, and so more active and lively, with fewer breathing problems, but owing to the slim waist and large head, many cannot whelp without veterinary attention and delivery by Caesarean section. The Frenchie remains somewhat of a specialist's breed, as there are also some hereditary eye problems.

The Boston Terrier is of entirely American breeding. Legend has it that the servants of wealthy citizens of Boston deliberately mated together their owners' pedigreed dogs, chiefly terriers and English and French Bulldogs, keeping the progeny secret, so that the Boston became the groom's or stableman's dog. Whelping is again a hazard in this breed and the prominent eyes are subject to injury. The Boston has the most pleasant temperament, being full of fun, clever and quick moving, and so makes a delightful pet.

The Poodles are meant to be sporting dogs, and the standards are still used for this purpose in France, especially to retrieve from water. Poodles are exceptionally intelligent, and perform the tasks they are taught with such joy and enthusiasm that they are often used in circus and stage shows. The Poodle had its height of popularity in the 1950s and 1960s, becoming at that time rather overbred, and so declining in health and temperament. A dog capable of being scissored and dyed, its nails varnished and curls tied up in bows, and still enjoying the process as much as its owner, will always have a popular following. Being so clever, the Poodle is also very sensitive, with nerves so finely balanced that they may easily be frightened by too much noise or boisterous play, so they are not the dog for a family of children, except possibly the standard Poodle, which is quite a large dog.

The Chow Chow worked in China, perhaps as a draught dog, but more usually as a dinner producer, as Chow Chow puppies were eaten as a delicacy. For some reason, the dignified Chow has never acknowledged itself as part of the stew, and still conducts itself with great reserve and true oriental inscrutability. Capable of great devotion to one owner, the Chow Chow never fusses or demonstrates abundant affection; it merely gives the impression that you are honoured to have its quiet, unflappable company.

A member of the spitz family, the Keeshonds were originally used as guards on canal boats of Holland and the Rhinelands. Still a very good traveller by train and car, it is the favoured pet of many families in Britain and USA as well as Scandinavia and Europe. The Keeshonds hearing is very acute, its character is pleasant but rather busy, and the bark is strong. Features of the breed are the deep-grey, shaded coat and the tightly curled tail.

This standard Schnauzer has the 'salt' colouring, the alternative being the yellowish brown or black 'pepper'. In USA a black and tan is also admitted to the standard. The harsh coat is easy to keep clean but requires hand stripping to preserve the smart outline, which should be nearly square with powerful, blunt muzzle.

Right
The Schipperke is a smart, small dog, short-backed and tailless. The head is decidedly foxy, with erect ears. The body coat and neck ruff is of dense hair, the legs comparatively smooth right down to the tiny feet. In USA and Europe black is the only colour allowed, but in South Africa and Britain, gold and cream shades are seen in the show ring.

Below
The very fox-like Finnish Spitz is often the beloved pet of those who like to ride to hounds. The colour should always be clear red, with very minimal white markings, dark eyes and black nose. When newborn, the puppies are greyish fawn, the coat clearing at weaning time.

The Schipperke is a native of Belgium, with something of the terrier in its features and a little pointed, foxy face, perhaps owing something to Pomeranian influence. Intelligent and bright, though not exactly beautiful, the Schip makes a good, if somewhat noisy housedog.

The Schnauzer is a dog of fairly recent German origin, made up of Poodle, Bouvier and German Shepherd Dog blood with touches of several other breeds, illustrating the fascination German breeders had for creating a custom-made dog. The word *schauzer* means 'snout', a fitting description for this dog with long head, square body and wiry beard and whiskers. The Schnauzer comes in giant, standard and miniature sizes, the latter being very popular housedogs in America. A hardy and long-lived breed, they are slow to mature and need firm handling when young.

The Tibetan dogs, the Shih Tzus, Lhasa Apsos, Tibetan Spaniels and Terriers, have been conserved for hundreds of years in the villages and monasteries of Tibet, and have spread to the western world comparatively recently. Now as pets they are probably the dogs of the future. The Tibetan Spaniels were said to have turned the prayer wheels in the monasteries. The validity of this is doubtful, but certainly the Tibetan breeds do tend to stand on their hind legs making movements with their 'hands'. All the varieties are 'watchers'; they will lie motionless for hours on window sills and the backs of chairs, eyes fixed on the

Left
This apricot toy Poodle bitch is in informal clip, as befits a matron nursing puppies. Poodles come in many colours, each shade having its own body characteristics. The apricot is one of the later shades to be developed, and is subject to some fading as the dog ages.

Above
The most popular colour in the Chow Chow is the red although black and blue follow closely. The beautiful cream shade with black eyes and points is rarely seen. The triangular foreface tapers from a broad head to a sharp muzzle with up-curving lips. Tongue, lips, and roof of mouth are black in all coat colours.

Right
The Poodle standard requires the dog to carry itself proudly, as this bitch does, her long neck holding the head high, and the tail pompom balancing the outline. This standard Poodle is in full lion clip, required for all show Poodles above one year old, but impossible to maintain in the companion dog. Notice the small tight feet so lightly poised on the ground.

distance, as their ancestors used to do, watching for travellers approaching from the monastery walls. Lhasa Apsos are very well established in USA, the original pair having been a gift from the Dalai Lama. The other Tibetan breeds are not yet recognized by the American Kennel Club, although they are by the British Kennel Club.

The Apso is heavily coated, needing a lot of grooming. Not very friendly with strangers, the Apso is a lively and hardy pet for the family, and reliable with children.

The Shih Tzu is of Chinese origin, much the same in shape and outline as the Apso, but with the fall of hair over the face tied back with a slide or a bow. For life entirely as a companion dog, the hair may be clipped short all over, which ruins the classic appearance but makes care easier. Particular features of this breed are the proud upright carriage of the head and the plumed tail. The American Kennel Club classifies the Shih Tzu among toy dogs.

The Tibetan Spaniel looks rather like a long-nosed Pekingese on longer legs. Originating as it does on the China/Tibetan border, there may have been some interbreeding long ago. The Tibetan Spaniel is very active, mischievous and very interested in all that goes on around its home in town or country.

The Tibetan Terrier was originally a herding dog, rather like a tiny Old English Sheepdog to look at, needing grooming to keep it in good condition for household life. Unfriendly with strangers, it is very loyal to its owners. All the Tibetans tend to have shrill, ringing barks, especially at the approach of visitors, and it is normal for them to shrink away from an extended hand until they know the caller well.

Left
The Tibetan Spaniel was bred in the mountain valleys bordering on China, and has quite a look of the Pekingese, but with straighter nose and longer in the leg. Many colours from cream through red to black are permitted. Eyes should be dark brown and nose black, although a 'pink' nose, as on the centre dog is not heavily penalized in the show ring.

Preceding pages
The name *apso* is said to mean goat-like and indeed the shaggy, rough coat of the Lhasa Apso is similar to that of an unkempt goat. The coat is very profuse, for protection at high altitudes, so the dog may shed it lavishly in hot weather in temperate climates. The Apso's tail is carried high over the back.

Above
The Tibetan Terrier is somewhat mis-named, as it has more sheep-herding than terrier characteristics. The head has a slight indentation, or stop, between the eyes, which are covered by a fall of hair. Coat colours are varied and intermingled from creams through greys, golds and black.

Toy dogs

The Shih Tzu is thought to be of Tibetan origin, and is in some ways akin to the Lhasa Apso, but this little dog has the shorter nose and the high head carriage so much prized in the Chinese Lion Dogs by the seventeenth-century emperors of China who followed the Buddhist religion and the tradition of worship of any dog shaped or coloured like a lion, because Buddha was said to have had a pet dog of this type. The coat is like human hair, varying in texture with the different colours. Gold shades predominate, and black and white is quite scarce.

The toy dogs are simply for pleasure, for amusement and enjoyment, for hot water bottles and tummy warmers, as well as for companionship. This is not to say that toy dogs are idle, indolent creatures that lie around all day. Many toy dogs are brisk walkers and keep busy around the house and garden all the time. Some that are miniaturized from working or gundog breeds still have working instincts and take great pleasure in following the activities of their larger ancestors. Toy dogs are very much attuned to their owners, and being of relatively small size, they may accompany their human to many places where a bigger dog would be in the way. Toys are still very much dogs, and require freedom and activity. They practise all the usual methods of dog communication, and they require sensible, balanced feeding, not chocolate and titbits all day. It is a pity, just because a dog is small, to ruin its teeth and digestion, and to pander and make a fool of it in a way that would be absurd in a bigger animal. Many of the toys have immense dignity and rather reserved natures. In some cases they are less demonstrative, and give less obvious affection than the Boxer or the Spaniel, and are less cuddly than the Golden Retriever, so in getting a toy dog, it is equally important to study natural temperament. The small are by no means all sweet.

The Pekingese has the unfortunate image of being spoilt, lazy and snappy. It is, in fact, a vigorous dog which enjoys a country walk and a game with children. Obstinate a Peke may be, but it is very intelligent and devoted. They are not wanderers or hunters, but very much enjoy watching the passing show from a window. Daily grooming is a necessity, giving particular attention to the eyes, which, being prominent, are apt to exude an excess of tears, and also are liable to injury if the Peke crosses swords with a cat. Very tiny specimens, known as 'sleeve Pekes' from being carried in the sleeves of Chinese garments, may be so small that the bitches may not be bred from. The Peke is one of the few breeds in which the bitch should be larger than the male.

The Yorkshire Terrier is another dog with a big personality in a small package. It has all the larger terrier's natural instincts, and is a superb ratter, but not, of course, while wearing the exaggerated length of hair that can be seen in the show dog. As a companion dog, the long silky coat can be trimmed down, allowing the dog to participate in any activity its owners choose, with the added bonus of it being easy to carry on public transport. The show Yorkie's coat demands infinite care; the darlings of exhibitors spend much of their time in curling papers, with exercise restricted to avoid breaking the hair. The Yorkie is an intelligent and observant dog, and has proved the answer to pet ownership for many people in Britain and USA.

The Silky Terrier sometimes known as the Sydney Silky is very reminiscent of the Yorkie, with something of the Skye Terrier ear carriage. The breed was produced by crossing the Yorkie with the heavier Australian Terrier. The Silky is not recognized by the British Kennel Club.

The Bichon Frisé is making a sudden bid for popularity both in Britain and the USA, and many people think this will be the star of the future, fulfilling as it does the answer to those owners who find Poodle upkeep too much of a problem. The

This Pekingese dog (*right*) is almost engulfed in its flowing coat with the plumed tail curling over the back. This amount of coat is necessary for a dog being exhibited. The red dog (*below*) has a more manageable coat length and is evidently a lively companion dog enjoying country life. The Peke should have a broad skull, flat and wide between the ears, a very short muzzle and be naturally undershot — that is, with the lower jaw protruding in front of the upper.

Right
The Yorkshire Terrier is in full show coat, the hair on the back being the much desired steel blue, although the tan on the head of this dog could be of richer colour. The eyes are correctly placed to look straight forward, and the bite should be even with no misplaced teeth. Yorkies in Britain are always shown mounted on small boxes to display the coat.

Bichon has been known on the continent of Europe for many centuries, being especially popular in Spain. These little dogs, which should not exceed 12 inches (30·5 centimetres) in height, are only lightly trimmed, and resemble a Poodle puppy all of their lives. At the moment the breed is scarce and expensive in Britain, but undoubtedly will become more abundant in time. The name is pronounced 'beeshon freezay' and translates roughly as 'curly spaniel'.

The Maltese comes from the same origins as the Bichon. It is a good-tempered, gentle little dog, remarkably free from hereditary faults and exaggerations, except for the length of coat desirable in the show dog. In the show style, the Maltese is beautiful but impractical for the pet owner to maintain. For everyday wear, the coat may be trimmed down, leaving just the head and tail hair full length. An attractive custom is to tie the topknot hair back in two plaits or with ribbon bows.

The Miniature Pinscher, familiarly known as 'Min Pins' is very like a tiny Dobermann, and stands about 12 inches (30·5 centimetres) high. They have the daring and audacity of the larger breed, considering themselves inferior to none, but the Min Pin makes rather more noise telling the world about it. A smart, clean-coated little dog, the Min Pin makes an active family pet.

The Lowchen, or Little Lion Dog, is a newcomer to both Britain and USA, although recognized in Europe for centuries. The coat is long and silky, and may be of any colour. The hair behind the ribs is usually clipped off leaving the head and front shaggy in the manner of a lion.

Right
The Bichon Frisé is a close-coupled little dog, with a broad, deep chest and a short back on stumpy legs. It is covered in a fine, white, woolly coat, and looks like a little teddy bear with black button nose and dark eyes. The temperament is cheerful and easy going, making it an engaging little pet dog.

Below
The Australian Terrier is not a toy dog, but makes its appearance here as the ancestor, through interbreeding with the Yorkie, of the Sydney Silky. The sturdy rough-coated Australian supplied size and height while the Yorkshire inheritance is the long and soft coat. Both breeds are basically blue and tan, so saving the risk of getting mismarked offspring in the new breed.

Right
There is nothing like a blue umbrella for flattering reflections! This Maltese is in beautiful show coat which, while it demands a lot of grooming, does not moult on the furniture. The nose, lips, eye rims and pads of the feet must be black, and the eyes dark brown.

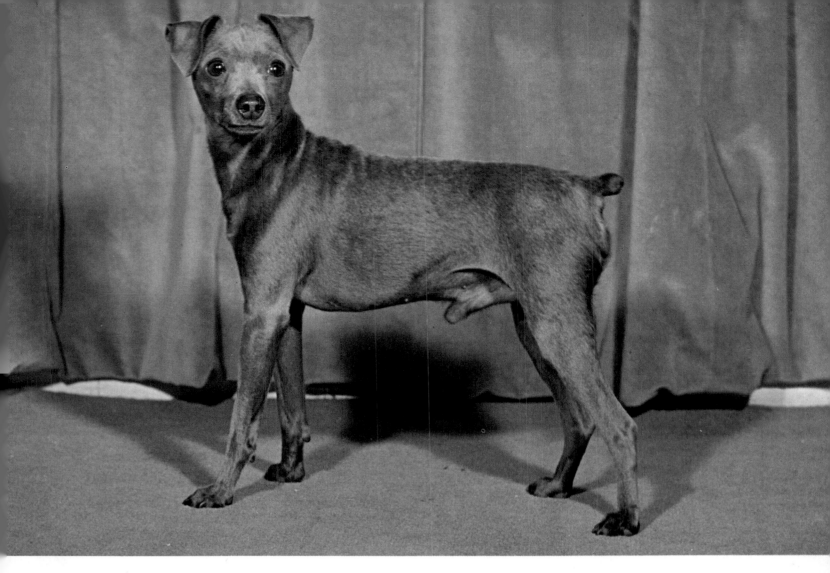

The Italian Greyhound is another miniature of a larger dog. It is elegant and beautiful, and not as delicate as its fine-boned appearance would suggest. This fastidious little dog likes warmth and comfort, and having such a fine coat, it makes an excellent indoor dog for the houseproud, as no mud is brought in on the tiny feet.

The Cavalier King Charles Spaniel finds itself a little out of place in the toy group, and many exhibitors would like it to be classed among the sporting dogs. Although the ideal weight is 15 pounds (6·8 kilograms), the majority of adult dogs weigh more and, if allowed, they delight in country exercise and putting up game. A shedder of coat and bringer in of mud on the feathered paws, this little dog nevertheless represents a useful compromise for many families who want a small dog that the men of the family are not ashamed to be seen with. An immense surge in popularity may have spoilt the temperament of some lines, but essentially the Cavalier is cheerful and easy going, everyone's friend and very adaptable, making holiday boarding easy. This breed is not noted for its intelligence, but makes up for this by being agreeable and generally as obedient as the average family would wish. The King Charles Spaniel is more rare, less active and rather less robust. It makes a charming pet for an older person, while the Cavalier is a children's dog. Originally springing from the same stock, the King Charles is now distinguished by its round, domed head and flat face, and like all breeds of that type, it must have nose folds and eyes kept clean, as well as the usual grooming of a silky coat.

The Japanese Spaniel is very popular in USA, but in Britain only some 200 a year are registered at the Kennel Club. Coat colour is predominantly white, so these dogs need frequent bathing or grooming with a dry shampoo powder, as the silky hair attracts dirt. The breed is lively and good-tempered, and has a stylish, high-stepping movement, very elegant on a dog which should weigh under 7 pounds (3 kilograms). It is highly suited to a town home, or even a flat, as is the Papillon. This breed comes in two forms: the Papillon with oblique ears, and the Phalene with drop ears. The Papillon (Butterfly Dog) is so-called because of the beautifully fringed ears, wide-spread like butterfly wings. These $5\frac{1}{2}$ to 6 pound (2·5 to 2·7 kilograms) dogs are hardier than their appearance would indicate, and they need a lot of exercise, unless they can be kept busy in a medium-sized garden. They are devoted to their owners, and have a very shrill bark to warn against intruders.

The Miniature Pinscher is proud, fearless and self-possessed, estimating itself second to none as the little dog in the picture shows. The colouring of this one is blue, a shade not recognized by the American Kennel Club, where deer-red is the preferred colour although black and chocolate are permitted. The close, smooth coat on these dogs is easy to care for.

Right
The Italian is a miniature Greyhound, slight, elegant and beautifully proportioned. The ears are rose shaped, well laid back but are actively mobile when the dog is listening. The neck is most gracefully arched, the chest deep and narrow, and the feet long as on all fast-running dogs.

Below
These Cavalier King Charles Spaniel puppies show three of the four colour varieties available – the black and tan, the ruby, and the red and white, known as the Blenheim. The fourth one is the tricolour and all these colours may appear in the same litter. The same four colours are found in the King Charles Spaniel. The ruby puppy has a faint white streak on the head which could spoil it for showing if it persists, and the black and tans should not have any white markings either.

Right
The King Charles Spaniel, known in USA as the English Toy Spaniel, is a compact little dog with a domed head, full eyes, short nose and upturned chin. The nose should be black, although at some times of the year, and during the bitch's reproductive cycle, the nose pigment will fade to brown. The coat is silky, without curl, and the tail is carried down.

The Pomeranian is another small and proud bundle of fur, sometimes as small as 3·5 pounds (1·6 kilograms). Queen Victoria set the seal of approval on these little dogs as pets, and also created a demand for them in America. While the Poms can be gay and amusing companions, the breed has lost some popularity because it can be both busy and noisy if not restrained. The Japanese, Papillon and Pom are more suitable for adults than for growing children.

The Pug is a long-term favourite pet and jester-dog. Clean of coat and rugged in character, like a little Mastiff, it has an excellent temperament and is fun with children. Like all the short-nosed breeds, the Pug snores, a warm and comforting sound, very soothing to hear in the night.

The Affenpinscher is very similar to the Griffon, but several pounds heavier, with an enormous wiry coat, and a little longer in the muzzle. Known as the monkey terrier, no one could call the Affenpinscher pretty, but it makes up for its looks in fearlessness and sturdy physique, although it is said to be somewhat excitable. There are rising numbers in America, but none are registered in Britain. In contrast, there are plenty of Griffon Bruxellois, which make splendid companions for older people, as they are very devoted to their owners, and are fascinating to watch, having such expressive, interesting faces. There are two coats, rough and smooth, and the roughs need hand-stripping twice a year.

The English Toy Terrier (Manchester) is a born ratter. Game, enthusiastic and devoted to its owner, it tends to be a one-man dog rather than a family dog, so it is more suited to adults than children. The Toy Terrier is an excellent house dog, the erect ears giving acute hearing, but these dogs must be curbed from hurling abuse at every passing dog and human, for they can easily become habitually noisy.

Below left
These Japanese Spaniels show the two colour variations in coat, with the desired, broad, white blaze between the eyes. An additional show point would be to have a small spot of colour in the middle of the blaze – the Buddha's thumbmark, said to have been made when blessing the breed. The head is large in proportion to the body, with the small ears set wide apart and high on the head.

Above
The Papillon shows to advantage the pretty, butterfly ears which give it its name. The body is that of a sound, balanced dog with no exaggerations. The head markings should be symmetrical, and the ears must be heavily fringed. Colouring is mainly white with trimmings of another colour.

Right
The Griffon is said to have a monkey face and the sturdy little dog here looks full of mischief. The turned-up chin is a feature of the breed, with dark eyes, black button nose and a deep stop between nose and skull. This rough-coated Griffon has a good wiry beard.

Above
This young Pomeranian shows the correct foxy expression on its wedge-shaped head. The neck is short on a deep chest, the coat being profuse and standing off from the body turning the dog into a ball of fur, on slight legs ending in tiny feet. A great range of colours is permissible.

Far right
This fawn Pug has all the clownish attributes of its kind, thoroughly enjoying doing a balancing act on the tightly curled tail which is such a desirable feature in the show dog. A Pug is now competing in working trials, clearing twice her own height in the high jump, showing that they can be quite an agile breed.

The Chinese Crested Dog is quite unique in the canine race, being almost hairless except for slight feathering on head, feet and tail. Parts of the skin are marked with leopard-like spots. The skin is warm to the touch, for like all dogs its natural temperature is higher than that of man, but the skin is a little rough, like the hands of a manual worker. A proportion of Chinese Crested puppies are born with coats, and an effort is being made to get this variety separately established as 'Powder Puffs'. At present they are unacceptable for show purposes and are usually destroyed by breeders. A cuddly dog, quiet and clean, the Chinese Crested is an ideal town pet.

The Chihuahua is the smallest toy dog of all, having an average weight of 4 pounds (1·8 kilograms), but some weigh much less, and cannot be bred from. This breed also has the advantage of being very long-lived, sometimes up to twenty years. There are two varieties, long- and smooth-coated. The smooths may throw long-coated puppies, but long coats bred together will not produce smooths. The Chihuahua is so small that he tends to find his dignity offended if grabbed at and drooled over by strangers. As a breed they are not superficially friendly, and can and will bite anyone who is over-familiar with them, especially when being carried by their owner. The Chi is quick moving and agile, and not so liable to accidental injury as one might suppose. However, care must be taken not to drop a Chihuahua, or to let it spring out of the arms or off a chair, as their fine bones are easily fractured. The Chihuahua is widely popular with flat dwellers and those with very small gardens. Do not buy a Chihuahua puppy from any establishment which keeps them in tiered cages, like rabbit hutches; the Chi needs freedom and exercise just like any other dog. Being so small, it is difficult to maintain soundness and straight front limbs if the dog's movements are restricted. Many Chihuahuas have a 'molera', a small opening on the top of the skull similar to the fontanelle in babies, which in the Chi often does not close, making the head very vulnerable to damage.

Above
The Chihuahua in the picture is smooth-coated, a compact, fine-boned little dog with well-springing ribs, nicely arched neck and straight front legs. The ears might be criticized for not being set low enough on the head. In the Chi, the tail may be carried sickle-wise, as this dog's is.

Left
This English Toy Terrier proudly holds its ears erect, which are correctly placed high on the head, and the eyes are the preferred almond shape. The body is compact with agile hindquarters and the tail is carried low. The tan markings are correctly placed; tan elsewhere on the body would be a serious show fault.

Right
The Chinese Crested has many pleasing features, being completely without doggy odour and having few hairs to shed. Many pastel skin colours are allowed, the natural tone seeming to be lilac mauve, darker in summer than in winter, with dark eyes, nose and lips.

Eyes always on its owner, responsive to a look, word or hand signal, this border collie at the 'down' waits only for the next command. Lively sometimes to the point of excitability, these dogs need activity and work to fill their day. The two dogs working together at a trials will manoeuvre the sheep in any direction with great expertise. A countryman will take great pride in owning a dog which shows off its good training, and also saves him a lot of leg work.

Other varieties

There are other dogs whose lineage and ancestry is carefully documented, but not at the kennel clubs, so they are not eligible for beauty shows. The foxhound and harrier packs come into this category. It is sometimes possible to obtain a puppy, or rather a couple, in these breeds, to 'walk' for the hunt, in the first summer of their lives. This relieves the hunt of the expense and labour of puppy rearing, and affords the hounds some experience of life outside the kennels. All these dogs will be friendly and genial with people but are almost sure to have an instinct to chase other animals. They must have plenty of free exercise and a warm stable or kennel to sleep in, so walking hounds is a country dweller's pursuit. The reward comes in taking your hounds to the puppy show where good rearing is apt to bring small prizes and probably an invitation to the point-to-point or the hunt ball. The foxhound and the harrier can be very beautiful, but they are not pets. Do not be persuaded that you can take surplus adults from a hunt pack and domesticate them, for it is just not possible and probably even cruel as the hound depends so much on its fellows for company and communication. Hounds are almost impossible to housetrain after many generations of kennel life.

A much more interesting and even more demanding type of 'walk' is to take a puppy destined to be a guide dog for the blind, or seeing eye dog in USA. Admirable as the society's training is, they freely admit that they cannot in any way provide the 'college education' which a puppy walker can give, and without which there would be no trained guide dogs. The breeds available will certainly be Alsatians, Labradors and Golden Retrievers, with a minority of other breeds and some crossbreeds, both dogs and bitches. These pups will go to the walkers at about eight weeks old or as soon as they have had their preventative inoculations. Families with children are preferred, and the dog must live in town surroundings or a busy suburb. A small maintenance allowance is made for the pup, and all veterinary bills are paid. The puppy walker undertakes to educate the dog to cope with every possible circumstance, to a much higher degree than that required of the normal pet, schooling the dog in every behaviour pattern from not stealing food to quelling barking and possessiveness. Walkers must take the dog on all kinds of transport, to schools, meetings and even jazz clubs, so that nothing comes as a shock to the guide puppy. Dogs at walk are only available in a limited number of areas, as they are assessed for progress at intervals by staff from the guide dog centres, and taken back for further tests and more specialized training at one year. The walkers may have first refusal if the dog fails to come up to standard, but many find a pride in knowing that they have started a successful guide dog on its way. This is a very worthwhile method of dog owning provided that all the family understands the relationship is only temporary, and that walking means dog training rather than having a permanent puppy to play with.

Some dog enthusiasts are glad that their dogs are not kennel club registered. The Jack Russell terrier and border collie breeders are among those divided in their ranks about being legitimatized, fearing that working ability will be lost if the breeds feature in beauty shows. Border collies should have work, for without it they can become neurotic and sad, as they are rather restless by nature. While a flock of sheep to chevy about is ideal, obedience work fills the need for many a border collie. They always take the top prizes in competitions as they carry out their work with such speed and accuracy. The border can be excitable, but will switch at once to being over-submissive, even downright subservient in attitude if corrected. Some owners will like this behaviour, while others will require more spirit and bravado in their dog. Border collies have some hereditary eye defects which are gradually being bred out by making an eye examination compulsory before the dog can take part in sheepdog trials.

The Jack Russell terrier is having a great wave of popularity, perhaps as an antidote to the cult of the pedigreed dog, but not all the short-legged terriers masquerading as Jack Russells are really entitled to that name. Parson Jack was a Victorian, the true sporting parson of the West country, who spent his weekdays fox hunting, taking special interest in the hunt terrier which was put down the hole after a bolted fox. Parson Russell defines his dog as being white (to distinguish it from the fox and the hounds) having a thick close jacket of wiry texture, with legs as straight as arrows, and about the size of a vixen. This is a very different dog from the bow-legged Corgi crosses one often sees labelled as Jack Russells today. There are some kennels breeding Jack Russells to type, and sometimes surplus puppies may be obtained from hunt kennels. There are classes for working terriers at some agricultural shows.

The lurcher is also a purpose-bred dog. It should be based on Greyhound or Whippet with some gundog blood, giving a fast game-killing dog which will also bring the prize home. Lurcher attributes are a lithe, svelte body; quietness; graceful movement and cryptic colouring. The ideal poacher's dog, it is somewhat wayward and used to an open-air life. One well-meaning rescue association took charge of a litter of lurchers abandoned by their travelling owners, only to find these dogs were often arriving back from their fine new homes, always on the run because they knew no boundaries, no enclosures, and having been reared on remote moorland, they had no traffic sense at all. The lurcher is a fine dog, if you have the right surroundings.

It is the pleasure of some people with ample resources of money and space to try

The foxhound is a pack animal. Singly they are friendly but not notably intelligent, collectively they are killers that will outwit any fox. One hound separated from the pack is miserable and lost, not capable of interpreting the scent pouring into its nostrils. Working capacity and the ability to give tongue are the judging points in the foxhound rather than colour or markings.

breeding experiments, either to infuse new blood into a declining breed, or to make an interesting cross which they think will provide the ideal dog for them. A complete outcross, say a Boxer bitch to a Dalmatian dog, with a view to improving hindquarters and gait in the Boxer line, will be able to be registered again at the Kennel Club as pure bred after three subsequent generations have been bred back to Boxer sires, but throwbacks to Dalmatian characteristics will occur for many more generations. In breeds which have improved quickly and become popular, there is often infiltration of other blood, used to bring down size or alter colour, so in litters for years after there will appear a puppy much larger, or smaller, blacker or straighter-nosed than its fellows. Such puppies should be registered as 'not to be bred from' and may command a small price as they are not typical of their breed. Unfortunately, it is not always possible to see such traits when the pup is at selling age.

Some breeds produce mismarked puppies which are not admissible to the show ring, and so will be available cheaply – for example, the white or checked Boxer, or the brown and white or black and white patched Poodle. These mismarks may be just as fine as pets, with all the character of their more conventional fellows, the only disadvantage being if the owner is slightly ashamed of not having a typical puppy, or values it less because it did not cost as much. Some pups are born with a wall eye, or an opaque eye, which is acceptable only in the Old English Sheepdog. These puppies can grow up to lead happy lives as pets. In gundogs, and in the Cavalier, breeders will sometimes have puppies with 'bad mouths', that is, undershot instead of the desired level bite. In the working gundog or the show Cavalier this matters, as an incorrect mouth can spoil the way the dog carries a bird. Such dogs make excellent working companions, their capacity to eat and the general health of their mouths being unimpaired, but they should not be used for breeding, in case the bad characteristic is passed on. More drastic physical ailments, such as hernias, lameness, hysterical behaviour, twitches and fits are not cheap at any price, nor is any dog with an unhealthy skin or an unresolved allergy, or a dog with bad temperament, worth considering.

Many people favour the mongrel dog, saying that the chance-bred hybrid has

The lurcher is very wise in country ways, both in tracking down a dinner and silently and swiftly killing it and bringing the prize home again. Powerful jaws, hindquarters cut up for speed and a long tail for balanced turning, and a keen eye are the requirements of the working lurcher.

Left
Blossom the Boxer bitch lacks the white head markings and collar trim, and she is too stocky in body to be worth entering in a beauty show, although she is sound in body and has excellent temperament. Mated to a tall, well-marked dog with excellent head, but slightly shy manner, Blossom produced a puppy which appears to be at this stage of very good shape with flashy markings, very confident in its bearing, showing the best of the attributes of both parents. However, many puppies fail to fulfil their early promise.

Right
This Boxer bitch has the customary Kennel Club registered pedigree but she is the ugly duckling of her family. Her badly shaped head is mismarked by the white patch extending right over one eye; her ears hang untidily; the shoulders are over-developed and the chest too wide. On the credit side, she is full of breed character, has an excellent short tight coat, although it is a little thin on the chest showing underlying skin pigment. She is abundantly healthy and clever, and the author's much loved 'Pooka'.

more self-reliance, and is more hardy than the pedigreed dog. This may in some measure be true, as the principles of survival of the fittest will often have to apply to the chance-bred dog whose conception and pregnancy may not have been under such favourable stars as the dog of planned breeding. The mongrel is a compound of all dogs, so perhaps getting back to the original dog which befriended man, showing the same attractions and the same gift for companionship without being dependent for every gesture on its master's will, as some highly bred dogs are. The mongrel has the chance to reproduce any virtues and vices, and so has a lucky dip in the pot of life. It runs true to the law of averages in that the mongrel is usually a medium-sized dog, with average dog ability and affections, not especially gundog, guard dog or lap dog. The crosses do seem to fall into types: the black retriever spaniel; the black and white collie cross; the shaggy coated white or yellow dog with sheepdog ancestors; the smooth-coated dog with feathering on ears and tail; and the fox terrier types. It is unusual to find a grey or blue shaded coat in the mongrel, or to see a short-nosed dog with up-turned chin. In crossing any of the short-nosed breeds, the nose feature is often lost in the first generation. Large and bulbous eyes, and pricked ears are also lost; eyes quickly revert to obliquely placed, almond-shaped eyes, and ears drop. The tail is usually long with a slight curve upwards, and the front legs are straight, not bowed.

With good food and care, mongrel puppies are likely to grow bigger than their parents, just as dogs taken from harsh climates where life is rough, overgrow the size stipulated by the kennel club standard in their native lands. The Hungarian sheepdogs now being imported are growing much bigger than their ancestors. Keeping dogs in a warm, centrally heated home may alter the texture of the coat, making it softer and more inclined to shed all the year round. Dogs which live outside in winter grow naturally thick coats and do not shed them until spring. Feet will become long and wide open in dogs living on carpet and grass, while the dog which lives in a concrete run, or walks a lot on the road, will have tight cat feet. All these elements may serve to alter your mongrel puppy, as well as its mixed heredity. Because the mongrel may have had less pre-whelping attention than the expensive pedigreed dog, it is always worthwhile having a veterinary surgeon look at the puppy at once, for worms and infectious disease. You owe this service both to the puppy and to your family, for children can catch some diseases from dogs which are not in the best of health.

Mongrels are usually very equable dogs, seldom fierce and usually very affectionate and enthusiastic about greeting their owner. If they may be said to have a fault it is their desire to be free. Their quick movements and sharp wits will aid them to make their escape, to join with others of their kind and go roaming, for mongrels are very gregarious. While many breeds of pedigreed dogs follow their owner closely as if fearing to get lost, the mongrel is often very self-reliant and shows no fear when exploring alone. Their desire to please makes the mongrel eminently trainable, and they often reach the top ranks in obedience trials. They will undertake all the orders given and carry them out with good heart, unlike the guarding breeds which do not enjoy the 'send away', as it is not in their instinctive behaviour to leave their owner and go out of sight, or the terrier, which does not take naturally to retrieving. Stripping and trimming, shortening whiskers and clipping nails does much to make a prettier outline on the mongrel, and you are not limited in beauty treatments by any breed club standards.

Mongrel or pedigreed, all dogs which we take into our homes will inevitably involve us in time and trouble, some dirt and damage, some loss of freedom, some expense, and some tears and heartbreak. Only you can say if the rewards make it worthwhile for your family.

Above
This wistful little terrier-type mongrel may reveal all kinds of hidden characteristics from its forebears. It will probably be clever, from many generations accustomed to fending for themselves, but also have an inbred instinct to be always on the move, somewhat independent of its owner's care.

Right
This is the shaggy type mongrel, perhaps having Collie or long-haired terrier ancestors. With good feeding, coat care and bathing such a dog may come to resemble many sheepdog breeds. Good feeding will make the dog grow to maximum size, and improves the coat texture.

Acknowledgments

Antarctica Shih Tzus – Ken and Betty Rawlings 76; Codach's Kennels 20T; Bruce Coleman Ltd – Hans Reinhard back jacket, back flap, 55 – Nicholas de Vore III 40–41B; Anne Cumbers 7, 9, 10T, 10B, 12, 13, 14, 16, 18T, 18B, 19, 21T, 21B, 22T, 22B, 24T, 24B, 27, 28T, 29BR, 30, 31L, 31R, 32T, 32B, 33, 35, 36, 37, 38, 39, 41TR, 41BR, 42–43, 44, 45T, 45B, 46–47B, 47BR, 50, 51B, 56T, 56B, 58TL, 58BL, 59, 60T, 60B, 61, 62, 63T, 65B, 66T, 66–67B, 69B, 70, 71B, 72–73, 74–75, 80TR, 80BR, 82C, 83L, 83R, 84L, 87, 88T, 90, 91, 92, 93; Neil Curtis 48; Tony Stone Associates Ltd front jacket; Sally Anne Thompson endpapers, title-page, 8, 11, 15T, 15B, 17T, 17B, 20B, 25, 26T, 26B, 28B, 29T, 29BL, 34T, 34B, 42L, 46–47T, 49T, 49B, 51T, 52, 53T, 53B, 57, 58R, 63B, 64T, 64B, 65T, 68, 69T, 71T, 75R, 78L, 78TR, 78BR, 79, 80L, 81, 82T, 82B, 84R, 85, 86T, 86B, 88–89B, 94, 95; Keystone front flap

Anne Cumbers and Sally Anne Thompson wish to thank the following owners and breeders for their kind co-operation: Mrs Ackerman 79; Mr and Mrs Alvi 51T; Mrs Baldry 65B; Mrs Banks 80TR; Mrs Barton 69T; Mrs Bentinck 78TR; Mrs Block 13, 21T; Mrs Boulton 33; Mrs Brackenbridge 72–73; Mr Butler 47BR; Miss Cartwright 44; Mrs Castle 7, 18B; Mrs Coy 56T; Mrs Craig 59; Miss Darby 25; Mrs Douglas-Redding 28B; Miss Edwards 74–75; Mrs Ellis 39; Mrs Elms and Mrs Elliott 42–43; Mrs Elsden 57T; Mr Fairclough 61; Mrs Farron Hill 66–67B; Mr and Mrs Fenski 32B; Mrs Field 24B; Mr and Mrs Fish 65T; Mrs Garrish 82T; Mrs Gilbert 38; Capt Grace 27; Mrs Green 30, 71T; Mrs Gregory 70; Mrs Hall-Jones 34T; Mrs Hammer 52; Mrs Harding 58BL; Mrs Harmar 86T; Mrs Harper 82B; Mrs Harten 58TL; Miss Hobbs 57; Mrs Holland 60B; Mr Holmes 78L, 94; Miss Humphries 81; Mrs Hunt 55; Mrs Hutchinson 37; Mrs Innes 22B; Mrs Jackson 58R, 60T; Mrs Jane 62; Mr Johnson 35; Mrs Khan 21B; Mrs Kirk 84R; Mr Lambert 91; Mrs Lanz 51B; Lady Lloyd 78BR; Mrs Lloyd 7; Mr Martin 88T; Mrs McGarvia 10T; Mr Mitchell 46–47T; Mrs Monckton 64T; Mr Muirhead 32T; Mrs Mulliner 101; Mr Norfolk 45T; Mrs Parker 87; Mrs Parkyns 49T; Mrs Perkins 26B; Miss Peter 83R; Mrs Piper 14; Miss Pockson 31L; Dr Poyner-Wall 22T; Mrs Price 69B; The Late Lord Rank 26T; Mrs Rampton 82C; Mrs Rees 9; Mrs Robinson 56B; Mrs Ross 49B; Mr and Mrs Scruby 41TR; Mrs Stringer 12; Miss Sully 83L; Mrs Swann 19; Miss Swyer 80L; Mr and Mrs A. Taylor 29T; Mrs Tidley 36; Mr and Mrs Tomlin 50; Mrs Tudor 29BR; Mrs Veasey 28T; Miss Vick 63B; Mr Walker 63T; Mrs White 46–47B, 92, 93; Mr and Mrs Willbie 64B; Mrs Wilkinson 24T; Mrs Williams 68; Miss Willis 16, 71B; Mrs Wilton-Clarke 17B; Mrs Woodrow 20B; Mrs Wynyard 29BL; Mr Zaboski 34B